D0094849

The PASSIONATE SHOPPER

The
PASSIONATE
SHOPPER

*Secret Sources for You
and Your Home*

Victoria

THE
EDITORS OF VICTORIA
MAGAZINE

TEXT BY
ANN LEVINE

HEARST BOOKS • NEW YORK

Copyright © 1999 by Hearst Communications, Inc.

All rights reserved. No part of this book may be reproduced
or utilized in any form or by any means, electronic or mechanical, including
photocopying, recording, or by any information storage or retrieval system,
without permission in writing from the Publisher. Inquiries should be
addressed to Permissions Department, William Morrow and Company, Inc.,
1350 Avenue of the Americas, New York, N.Y. 10019.

It is the policy of William Morrow and Company, Inc.,
and its imprints and affiliates, recognizing the importance of preserving
what has been written, to print the books we publish on acid-free
paper, and we exert our best efforts to that end.

Library of Congress Cataloging-in-Publication Data
The passionate shopper: secret sources for you and your home.
p.   cm.
ISBN 0-688-16737-3
1. Shopping Guidebooks.
TX335.P362   1999
640'.73—dc21   99-23391
CIP

Printed in the United States of America

First Edition

1 2 3 4 5 6 7 8 9 10

BOOK DESIGN BY LEAH LOCOCO

www.williammorrow.com
www.victoriamag.com

"BORN TO SHOP" states one of the handsomely stitched needlepoint pillows prominently displayed in a favorite shop of ours, and here at *Victoria,* we take these words to heart. Just like you, we are passionate about shopping—it is one of our favorite pastimes. Every year in our August issue, we bring some of our delightful finds to your attention. By now, our little black book is quite full of names and addresses telling us where to go for just the right fashion accessory or for special furnishings for home and garden. With all the wonderful crafters and collectors we've come to know through our pages, we thought it was time to share our favorite finds and secret sources in an easy-to-use book—a directory that makes shopping more convenient and enjoyable than ever.

Inspired by the thought of building a business from the ground up, these designers and shop owners have undertaken a creative endeavor and succeeded. It is our pleasure to introduce them to you; they have followed their dreams by pursuing a vision—and they have captured many a shopper's heart and soul.

On these pages, we've assembled a sampling of shops and resources we consistently rely on—some for the prettiest spring hats, others for the most delicious cakes, still others for luxurious linens and unusual antiques. For some of the businesses a phone number rather than an address is given, and we encourage you to call first for more information. Whatever the wares, we know you'll find them wonderful.

NANCY LINDEMEYER

Editor in Chief, Victoria *magazine*

CONTENTS

CONTENTS

For

YOUR HOME

Antiques

ANIMAL ART ANTIQUES

617 Chartres Street

New Orleans, LA 70130

(504) 529-4407   animalart@msn.com

England's Queen Victoria and Prince Albert had a deeply felt love of animal art, a tradition that is honored at Charlie and Sue Murphy's Animal Art Antiques in New Orleans. This unique shop features portraits and sculptures of beloved pets from the past—in needlepoint, stained glass, porcelain, and papier-mâché.

APIARY

585 Milwaukee Street

Denver, CO 80206

(303) 399-6017

Mother Nature plays a big role at this antiques-filled shop. Owner Jean Snow has long been enthralled by flora and fauna, and the silver, china, linens, and artwork she collects and carries abound with bird and botanical motifs.

BRYONY TOMASSON

283 Westbourne Grove

Portobello Market

London W11 4UP England

(011) 44 171 731 3693 (Saturdays only or by appointment)

This London antiques shop helps create an awareness of the beauty, value, and worth of humble everyday objects such as linens, handmade quilts and covers, homespun yarns, hand-stitched clothes, and old buttons. These and other rustic items from the villages of England and France are for sale here by an owner who treasures the simple colors and textures of nineteenth-century country life.

BUNGALOW

4 Sconset Square/15 Myrtle Avenue

Westport, CT 06880

(203) 227-4406

After accompanying her mother-in-law on buying trips to England, shop owner Wende Cohen turned a private passion for antiques into an artful business. Wende is partial to unusual accessories—hand-painted bowls, crystal, vases, wire birdhouses, and bamboo tables—that pull a room together.

FRIEND OR FAUX

28 Earsham Street

Bungay, Suffolk NR35 1AQ England

(011) 44 1986 896170

Returning to her native England after years spent living in Canada, Jane Cudlipp found her true calling when she and her daughter Kim Sisson opened a store filled with a medley of cherished antiques and collectibles.

LYME REGIS

68 Thompson Street

New York, NY 10012

(212) 334-2110

or

43 North Main Street, Kent, CT 06757

"I love curiosities that surprise or befuddle," says shopkeeper Elaine Friedman, who finds many of her treasures on travels to England. In fact, with its fashionable accessories, amusements, and souvenirs of times gone by, Elaine's SoHo store resembles an olde curiosity shoppe of yore.

MARSTON HOUSE

Main Street, P.O. Box 517

Wiscasset, ME 04578

(207) 882-6010

Famous for its picturesque setting, the seaside town of Wiscasset, Maine, is also known for its quaint main street, home of Marston House Antiques. Marston House occupies a meandering old house that springs to life when owners Sharon and Paul Mrozinski fill it with their fascinating collection of treasures for home and garden.

OUTSIDE INN

P.O. Box 135

Wallingford, PA 19086

(800) 527-8864   outsid@aol.com   www.outside-inn.com

The outdoors steps in at this romantic antiques shop, filling it with flower-strewn hand-painted furniture, rose arbors, picket fencing, carved wooden leaves, and more—all adapted for delightful indoor use.

POOTER OLOOMS

339 State Street

Harbor Springs, MI 49740

(616) 526-6101 (Saturdays only or by appointment)

Jenny Feldman's Michigan shop promises and delivers whimsical furnishings as fanciful as the store's name. Most of the unusual wares at Pooter Olooms travel from Europe, where Jenny is always on the lookout for merchandise—armoires, lamps, clocks, chairs— from different eras to fill her store.

RUBY BEETS

1703 Montauk Highway

Bridgehampton, NY 11932

(516) 537-2802

Mailing address: P.O. Box 596, Wainscott, NY 11975

American antiques fill the eight rooms of this easygoing Long Island shop, a former home dating to 1790. Owners Sharone Einhorn and Honey Wolters claim they can easily furnish whole houses with the pieces on display at Ruby Beets—from beds to cupboards to ironstone.

SALLEA

66 Elm Street

New Canaan, CT 06840

(203) 972-1050   www.artnet.com/sallea.html

Containers crafted of fine wood, precious tortoiseshell, gleaming silver, delicate ivory, and subtle mother-of-pearl are the specialty at Sallea Antiques. Owner Sally Kaltman collects boxes of all shapes and sizes, most of them from the eighteenth and nineteenth centuries, to fill her New Canaan, Connecticut, shop.

TUDOR ROSE

28 East Tenth Street

New York, NY 10003

(212) 677-5239

If you're looking for antique sterling silver, you'll do no better than to begin the search at Tudor Rose, where vanity pieces, tableware, frames, candlesticks, and vases vie for space in this tiny New York City storefront. English and American designs make up the better part of the collection with an emphasis on Victorian-era pieces.

WIDOW DAVIS ANTIQUES

2906 Route 209

Kingston, NY 12401

(914) 339-0600

Housed in a stone structure that owner Alan Brasington believes is one of the oldest in New York, Widow Davis Antiques is a stroll through history. The antiques and decorative accessories Alan and partner Rita Lutsky sell are appealingly assembled in homey arrangements that evoke the best of past and present.

China/Tableware

AS YOU LIKE IT

3025 Magazine Street

New Orleans, LA 70115

(800) 828-2311   ayliss@cris.com   www.cris.com-ayliss

Heirloom silver holds a special tradition and grace that comes only with age. Dealer Helen Cox appreciates this cherished patina so much that she collects only antique pieces for her New Orleans shop As You Like It. Some of her favorite vintage pieces include loving cups, salvers, sugar bowls, servers, and saltshakers.

....

COUNTRY DINING ROOM

178 Main Street

Great Barrington, MA 01230

(413) 528-5050

China, silver, and glassware like this are rarely seen under one roof, say fans of Country Dining Room's extensive collection of antique tableware. Rare pieces from the past—majolica, transferware, lusterware, pressed glass, compotes, pastry stands—are Sheila Chefetz's stock-in-trade. She combs flea markets and antiques stores wherever she travels to maintain her outstanding assortment.

....

CRAVEN POTTERY

1692 Highway 80 South

Micaville, NC 28755

(800) 764-2402

Pressed into the surface of Ian and Jo Lydia Craven's pottery is patterned lace that leaves a lasting impression on the plates, platters, and pitchers they produce in their North Carolina studio. The Cravens use heirloom laces to create beautifully textured tableware pieces.

....

EARTHLY POSSESSIONS

10 Bassett Street

Milton, MA 02186

(617) 696-2440

Collectors Sandy and Ken Keohane don't have as much interest in matched sets of china as they do in sensational single pieces they can pair with almost anything. They're fond of mixing Wedgwood with Spode, lilies with lilacs, nineteenth century with twentieth— and do so with much aplomb at their Milton, Massachusetts, store.

EMMA BRIDGEWATER

739 Fulham Road

London SW6 5UL England

(011) 44 171 371 9033

bridge.water@btinternet.com   www.bridgewater-pottery.co.uk

Taking advantage of centuries-old kilns in Stoke-on-Trent, England, local artist Emma Bridgewater designs pottery sprinkled with charming spongeware motifs. This well-made tableware is decorated with fruits, flowers, and flowing letters that scamper across the rims of plates, teacups, mugs, and saucers.

HÔTEL

47 Cedar Gate Road

Darien, CT 06820

(203) 655-4252

To see a piece of Ginger Kilbane's vintage tableware is to be reminded of the days when traveling in grand style meant hotels,

ships, and trains with tables set with fine linens, china, and silver for every meal. Her table accessories come from the great hotels, railroads, and cruise lines of Europe, collections that carry a patina from the past.

....

LARK RODERIGUES

73 West Passage Drive

Portsmouth, RI 02871

(401) 683-5298 (by appointment only)

This gifted artist finds fresh inspiration in every flower that grows, carefully sculpting and painting her creations to bloom on bowls, plates, pitchers, and vases. Lark's pottery pieces are all hand thrown, then embellished with free-flowing florals. She first sketches her designs on unglazed earthenware pieces with a pencil, then turns to her palette of paints to bring her flower renderings to colorful life.

....

LUCULLUS

610 Chartres Street

New Orleans, LA 70130

(504) 528-9620

Lucullus is not only a treasure trove of antique tableware, it is a study in dining history. By examining cooking, eating, and dining habits from the past, owner Patrick Dunne has developed a finely honed appreciation of antique tableware. From pewter spoons to porcelain tea sets, crystal glasses to printed menu cards, Lucullus unveils proper etiquette from the well-mannered past.

....

MACKENZIE-CHILDS

3260 State Route 90

Aurora, NY 13026

(212) 570-6050 or (315) 364-7123

Enchanting, endearing, expressive—these are the words that best describe the pastel pottery of two creative artists who celebrate their vision of home through their work. Victoria and Richard MacKenzie-Childs produce plates, cups, tiles, and goblets with lighthearted tartans and checkerboards. Such whimsical work brightens any cupboard or table.

....

MARY ROSE YOUNG POTTERY

11 Walcott Street

Bath BA1 5BN England

(011) 44 1225 445899   maryroseyoungmcmail.com

A garden blooms within the walls of Mary Rose Young's shop in Bath, England. Roses top teapots, line shelves, and embellish vases, each one carefully crafted to add a floral flourish to Mary Rose's pretty pottery. As Mary Rose's art develops, she finds her designs focus more and more strongly on her namesake flower.

....

MEISSEN SHOP

329 Worth Avenue

Via Roma 5

Palm Beach, FL 33480

(561) 832-2504

The very first porcelain ever manufactured in Europe, Meissen is especially decorative and full of flourishes. At this Palm Beach shop, all sorts of hand-painted showpieces are for sale: clocks, vases, sconces, and statues, all originating from Germany in the eighteenth century.

NICHOLAS MOSSE POTTERY

Bennettsbridge

County Kilkenny, Ireland

(011) 353 56 27505   www.nicholasmosse.com

The pride of Kilkenny, Ireland, Nicholas Mosse's pottery reflects the many charms of the countryside from which it is produced. Traditional spongeware techniques are used to create tableware designs that mix winsome patterns with cheerful colors.

SIMON PEARCE

The Mill

Quechee, VT 05059

(802) 295 2711

This former woolen mill in the tiny village of Quechee, Vermont, now produces radiant blown glass and gleaming pottery, all made by crafters who work within well-established Irish traditions. These elegantly simple pieces, overseen by designer Simon Pearce, are highly acclaimed for both their form and their function.

SPODE LIMITED

Church Street

Stoke-on-Trent ST4 1BX England

(011) 44 1782 744 011

Founded over two centuries ago by Josiah Spode, the company that still carries his name produces tableware featuring patterns and pictures that tell of nature, village life, families, and early English history. In 1784 the company perfected the art of transferring intricate engravings from copperplate to dinner plate, giving Spode its signature look.

Decorative Finishes/Paint

JOE CANTO FINE ART

P.O. Box 4403

Allentown, PA 18105-4403

(610) 820-0977

($10 catalog available; refundable with first purchase)

Simple wooden antiques are magically transformed into showpieces when embellished with Joe Canto's decorative additions. This accomplished craftsman restores old furniture; adds a distressed finish; then places cupids, rosettes, swags, and garlands in pleasing arrangements on drawers and doors.

MARY BORGEN

1732 Front Street

Slidell, LA 70458

(504) 649-8153

In artist Mary Borgen's own words, "Everything could do with a posy or two." This aptly explains the beautifully painted finishes that adorn her furniture, jewelry boxes, trunks, and floor cloths. In her Louisiana studio, Mary paints garden flowers, garlands, and bows that grace once-plain wooden surfaces.

....

FIRED EARTH

Twyford Mill

Oxford Road

Adderbury, Oxon OX17 3 HP England

(011) 44 1295 81 2088

Antique paint colors inspired by rich hues once made from natural earth pigments are the specialty of this English design firm. No matter how they're used, these historic colors, developed in consultation with the Victoria and Albert Museum, create a stunning palette on woodwork and walls.

....

STONEHOUSE FARM GOODS

544 West Water Street

Princeton, WI 54968

(888) 382-4500 or (920) 295-4500

Tracy and John Porter, owners of Wisconsin's Stonehouse Farm Goods, are so at home with nature that they borrow the best of woodland motifs to adorn their hand-painted furniture. From their studio workshop come desks, tables, armoires, and chairs covered in floral and fauna designs richly rendered in painted tableaux.

Fabrics

BENNISON FABRICS

76 Greene Street

New York, NY 10012

(212) 941-1212

fax: (212) 941-5587

Carefully reproducing wonderful prints from the past— and leaving the antique "faded" quality intact—Bennison Fabrics are known for a subtle, muted palette. The soft colorations work well at windows, on furniture, as pillows—all throughout a room.

GETCHELL'S

5012 Xerxes Avenue South

Minneapolis, MN 55410

(612) 922-6222

Since Linda Getchell has always loved fine fabrics, it seems only fitting and natural that her Minneapolis, Minnesota, shop specializes in cabbage-rose prints, textured bark cloths, and other vintage textiles so prized by Midwestern farm families of the 1930s and 1940s. In her tiny store, these pristine pieces of cloth are transformed into pillows, panels, bedding, and tablecloths.

MOTIF

20 Jones Street

New Rochelle, NY 10802

(800) 431-2424

    Beautiful fabrics are not only Lyn Peterson's passion, they're her business. As head of design for Motif, she creates fine fabrics that are inspired by classic patterns of the past but hold up well in terms of today's tastes and needs. Lyn sees pattern in everything and enjoys bringing a compatible mix into every room of the home.

NINA CAMPBELL

7 Milner Street

London SW3 2QA England

(011) 44 171 589 8589

    An unerring eye for freshness and simplicity marks Nina Campbell's fabrics. Always meeting her own standards for good taste, charm, and comfort, Nina designs fabrics in patterns and colors that combine easily in a variety of settings. Her inventive fabric uses and ideas have helped give English country-house style such desirable cachet.

PAPER WHITE

P.O. Box 956

Fairfax, CA 94978

(415) 457-7673

    The interplay of pattern and light is a guiding force for designer Jan Dutton as she creates fabrics that can serve many purposes and function in many ways. Her cottons, voiles, linens, and damasks can dress a bed, drape a table, frame a window, or fill many a need, especially in the bedroom and bath.

....

VIRGINIA DISCIASCIO ANTIQUE TEXTILES

19 East Seventy-first Street

New York, NY 10021

(212) 794-8807

Imagine layers of vintage fabrics beautifully draped and displayed all ready for browsing or buying. That's what you'll find when you visit Virginia's studio, featuring a world-class collection of fine linens and textiles.

....

WAVERLY

(800) 423-5881

Waverly, one of America's most esteemed design resources, outfits each of its home stores with fabrics and furnishings so comfortable, shoppers feel like invited guests in a private home. The cozy room ensembles showcase paints and wall coverings all designed to mix and match with a range of Waverly products.

....

WHITCHURCH SILK MILL

28 Winchester Street

Whitchurch, Hampshire RG28 7AL England

(011) 44 125 689 3882

The last such mill in England, Whitchurch Silk Mill turns out yard upon yard of moirés, taffetas, and organzas befitting everything from wedding gowns to judges robes. This English factory has been in production for over 165 years, dedicating itself to the history of the mill as well as the beautiful fabrics that can be produced only by skilled weavers.

Framers

DL RHEIN

318 West Ninth Street, #310

Los Angeles, CA 90015

(213) 624-7673

fax: (213) 624-5144

After several successful years selling decorative picture frames, business owner Deborah Rhein doesn't have to choose between frame or fortune. Her popular designs allow her both. The line offers a range of sizes and styles, some ribbon-trimmed, others covered in pretty pearls, still others handsomely embellished with dried rosebuds.

ELEMENTS

www.elementsjillschwartz.com

Stylish picture frames are the specialty of former graphic designer Jill Schwartz, who brings her whimsical sense of design to each piece she imagines. While some frames might incorporate buttons and beads, others carry creative painted finishes.

FRANK AND JOE GALLERY

328 East Seventy-eighth Street

New York, NY 10021

(212) 535-0167

Large, small, old, new—if it's frames you're looking for, you'll find them here. The selection is extensive and the possibilities are endless, from fully customized to "off the rack."

GILL & LAGODICH PERIOD FRAMES & RESTORATION

108 Reade Street

New York, NY 10013

(212) 619-0631   gillagod@ix.netcom.com

Collecting and restoring antique frames is the mutual calling of collectors Tracy Gill and Simeon Lagodich, who find irresistible beauty in gilded glories of yore. With painstaking care, these two restoration experts determine just how to treat each frame they find by establishing its origin, history, and age. Most of their frames date from the nineteenth century, carrying an interesting amount of period detail and ornamentation.

YESTERYEAR

8816 Beverly Boulevard

West Hollywood, CA 90048

(310) 278-2008

Yolanda Tisdale's Los Angeles frame shop is filled with prints, portraits, and paintings she elegantly frames for maximum effect.

And that's not all customers find gracing her walls. Fabrics, laces, sketches, souvenirs, and botanicals are all suitable for framing, Yolanda believes, and she does so with creativity and imagination.

Furniture

ANANDAMALI

35 North Moore Street

New York, NY 10013

(212) 343-8964

fax: (212) 343-2544

Every piece of Cheryl Hazan's furniture has a story to tell. Her sideboards, cabinets, and coffee tables are covered in bits and pieces of broken china, a surface decoration called *picassiette*. Cheryl's signature look is a careful arrangement of china pieces on furniture, garnering undivided attention and nonstop comments.

BOMBAY COMPANY

(800) 829-7789

Lavish vignettes and dazzling displays are hallmarks of the Bombay Company stores and catalogs. Pieces from this exclusive furniture collection, which constantly changes, include romantic beds, stately tables, comfy chairs, and versatile desks. Special themes and a variety of smaller accessories keep customers interested—and coming back.

DREXEL HERITAGE

101 North Main Street

Drexel, NC 28619

(800) 916-1986 or (704) 433-3200   www.drexelheritage.com

Aptly named to emphasize its commitment to respecting the times and tastes that have preceded ours, Drexel Heritage draws on designs from the past for its furniture collections. Well-crafted tables, chairs, desks, and beds are enduring—in terms of both quality and style.

GRANGE

200 Lexington Avenue, 2nd Floor

New York, NY 10016

(800) GRANGE-1   www.grange.fr

Simplified furnishings whose lines speak of earlier times blend well with antiques yet have a contemporary ease. That's the fresh spirit of Grange furniture, an innovative company that promotes timeless decorating as their design philosophy.

HABERSHAM

P.O. Box 1209

Toccoa, GA 30577

(800) 241-0716   www.habershamplantation.com

Habersham is known for applying artistic painted finishes to furniture pieces ranging from beds to benches, settles to settees. Styles include American primitive, romantic European, and country cottage, all painted and finished by hand.

HICKORY CHAIR

(800) 349-HKRY

A company noted for its attention to period detail, Hickory designs work well with furnishings both formal and informal because the lines are so wonderfully pure and simple.

HIGHLAND HOUSE

(888) 831-5313   www.highlandhousefurn.com

It's not necessary to be in England to enjoy the Cotswold cottage look. Thanks to furniture designs by Highland House, this romantic mood can be captured in homes everywhere. Sofas, loveseats, and chairs lend a casual sophistication to any room.

LEXINGTON

(800) LEX INFO

Unassuming heirlooms expertly crafted and finely conceived are the signature of Lexington Furniture Company. The designs—graceful but not grand—are both decorative and serviceable, putting good looks and practicality to work.

LILLIAN AUGUST

22 Elizabeth Street

South Norwalk, CT 06854

(203) 454-0675

Furniture that wraps its arms around you in friendly comfort is the province of Lillian August, lending welcome-home atmosphere to every room. Designing pieces that are comely and shapely, the furniture invites you to come and sit for a spell on sofas and chairs that warm a room with style.

....

MAINE COTTAGE

P.O. Box 935

Yarmouth, ME 04096

(207) 846-1430   www.mainecottage.com

Fun furniture designs embellished with whimsical details and finished in bright colors are the specialty at Maine Cottage. No matter what style best describes your own "cottage," you'll find beds, desks, hutches, and armoires that fit your decorating scheme.

....

SAMPSON BOG

171 Paradise Point

Mayfield, NY 12117

From a secluded studio deep in the Adirondack Mountains, Barney and Susan Bellinger design one-of-a-kind furniture built of native woods and enhanced with hand-painted scenes of nature. Outfitted in delightful detail with pinecones, acorns, twigs, and bark, each piece, including chests, desks, cabinets, and tables, carries the name Sampson Bog, in honor of a favorite fishing spot. Send $13.50 for a catalog.

....

SHABBY CHIC

(800) 876-3226

Rachel Ashwell, founder of Shabby Chic stores, has a unique ability to combine sophistication with livability, a talent immediately noticeable to visitors browsing through the easy mix of slipcovered furniture found in her shops. Whatever Rachel finds or creates, she marries the casual with the elegant for a stylish, comfortable look with lots of character.

....

SUMMER HILL

2682H Middlefield Road

Redwood City, CA 94063

(650) 363-2600

Fanciful furniture by Summer Hill draws on designer Rela Gleason's memories of places she has loved. She remembers a playhouse, a clapboard cottage, a vacation home in New England, and combines them all to create a line of upholstered chairs, tufted chaise lounges, and whitewashed beds that resemble some of her prized family heirlooms.

....

SWEDISH BLONDE

P.O. Box 4430

Archdale, NC 27263

(800) 274-9096   www.swedish-blonde.com

Designer Ann Milläng uses the simple elegance of Sweden's Gustavian furniture as the primary source of inspiration for her Swedish Blonde furniture company. In re-creating pieces as enduring as the originals, Ann uses softly painted patinas and hardy woods to share the classic timelessness of her line with a new generation.

....

WHISPERING PINES CATALOG

43 Ruane Street

Fairfield, CT 06430

(800) 836-4662

Furnishings from the family tree is how Whispering Pines owners Mickey Kelly and Susan Panian describe their all-American mix of furniture and accessories. With a cabin-related theme filling the pages of their catalog, Mickey and Susan either design or find lighthearted desks, chairs, ottomans, and couches that evoke a nostalgia for the past while securing a lasting place in homes of the present.

Home Furnishings

AMBROSIA'S GARDEN

1204 East Atlantic Avenue

Delray Beach, FL 33483

(561) 272-9860

It takes a dyed-in-the-wool antiques lover to assemble the comfortable, compatible mix found at Ambrosia's Garden, and owner Ambie Hay proudly admits her passion. Ambie gathers pillows, baskets, rugs, and paintings that give her Florida shop its softly romantic look and feel.

BLUE RACCOON

6 Coryell Street

Lambertville, NJ 08530

(609) 397-1900

New Jersey's ever-changing Blue Raccoon is a shop filled with the homey, the handmade, and the unusual. Walking into this creative mix is always a pleasure for customers, even the regulars who never quite know what to expect.

BOUNTIFUL

1335 Abbot Kinney Boulevard

Venice, CA 90291

(310) 450-3620   bountiful@earthlink.net

This aptly named store in Southern California is renowned for a profusion of unique merchandise and collectibles. Owner Sue Balmforth has turned Bountiful into the decorating destination of choice for homeowners looking for unusual antiques.

CACHET COLLECTION

P.O. Box 2747

Manchester Center, VT 05255

(802) 362-0058   fax: (802) 362-5221

Full of ideas and inspiration, Cachet Collection is a store that brings a fresh point of view to antique home furnishings while inventing new ways to use fabrics and accessories. Owners Judy Rosley and Nancy Hagen suggest an interplay of seasoned favorites with choice purchased pieces to create a renewed sense of place.

CHEZ GRAND'MÈRE

24 Tinker Street

Woodstock, NY 12498

(914) 679-8140   www.enjoyhv.com/chezgrandmere

Under Misty Lucas's careful eye, goods and goodies imported from France always find their way to Chez Grand'mère. Faience, Quimper, and other wares from the regions of Provence, Anjou, and Loire are favorites of both the shop owner and her customers.

DEANNA YOUHANNA

P.O. Box 16263

Beverly Hills, CA 90209

(310) 550-0052 (by appointment only)

In a design business that bears her name, Deanna Youhanna shares her taste for decorative European and American antiques with a stylish mix of china, linens, furniture, and paintings. Deanna's artful touches change frequently, but clients can always count on a cheerful combination of pattern and color.

FIREHOUSE ON CHURCH STREET

19 Church Street

New Milford, CT 06776

(860) 355-2790

Unusual finds and good company always await visitors who shop the Firehouse on Church Street. Owner Gaye Parise turns customers into friends as they peruse the store's ever-changing selection of home fashions and furnishings.

....

FRENCH LACE

17 South State Street

Newtown, PA 18940

(215) 579-6956

Relying on her background in fine arts, shopkeeper Nina Kaplan makes sure every corner of her store is carefully composed. Filled with furniture, tableware, and antique accent pieces, French Lace leaves an artistic impression on the hearts and minds of its customers, who take home wonderful wares from Nina's "gallery."

....

HOMESTEAD

223 East Main Street

Fredericksburg, TX 78624

(830) 997-5551

"Little lifestyles stores, each with its own story to tell" is how Carol Bolton describes the shops that have sprouted from Homestead, her Fredericksburg, Texas, flagship. Homestead continues to carry a wide range of antiques and home furnishings, while the smaller shops cluster around themes such as gardening and children.

....

INDIES LANDING, INC.

515 Park Avenue North

Winter Park, FL 32789

(407) 740-8444 indies@earthlink.net

At Indies Landing, owner Anne Burst mixes dashing elements of Colonial style for a look that is at once informal and classic. Imports from the British West Indies combine with antique rattan, bamboo, and raffia for an easy elegance that suggests tea on the veranda.

IVY HOUSE

High Street, Rode

Bath BA3 6NZ England

(011) 44 1373 830013 (by appointment only)

fax: (011) 44 1373 830160

When picturing English style, certain images come to mind: soft sofas and pillows, generous curtains, solid antiques, plush area rugs. All this and more is available at Ivy House, where the shop owners are so adept at styling this comfortable look, they even hold design workshops for clients hoping to bring this look to their own homes.

JANIS ALDRIDGE

2900 M Street NW

Washington, DC 20007

(202) 338-7710

or 50 Main Street, Nantucket, MA 02554

(508) 228-6673

A fresh vision of tradition is what Janis Aldridge offers at her

Washington, DC, shop. The pillows, plates, lamps, and tea sets make an artful assemblage in this private parlorlike setting. Janis's finds concentrate on antique treasures that are as at-home in this quiet Georgetown neighborhood as she is.

....

LIBERTY

1295 Seymour Street
Vancouver, BC V6B 3N6 Canada
(604) 682-7499

The tastes of a mother and daughter-in-law combine beautifully at Liberty, a Vancouver shop full of decorative finds. Architects and designers love Liberty for its air of casual elegance. Fruit, flowers, and fountains blend with the subdued color scheme: Most of the merchandise is white, black, gray, or silver. The truly old mixes with the "new-with-patina" for an artful assortment.

....

ORNAMENTA

235 Main Street
Northport, NY 11768
(516) 757-2949

This nature-inspired shop on New York's Long Island flowers in every season. Vintage vases, floral potpourris, and objets d'art are not just your garden-variety antiques. These are handpicked by owners Jane McGowan and Catherine Benincasa to bring the natural world indoors.

....

PUTTI

1104 Yonge Street

Toronto, Ontario M4W 2L6 Canada

(416) 972-7652

Enticing window displays of vintage textiles, European antiques, flower-filled urns, and plump pillows invite shoppers to experience the warmth of Putti, a romantic find on Toronto's bustling Yonge Street. "Oh, I could move right in," customers tell owners Linda Wade and Martin Dwyer, which these former corporate businesspeople take as the ultimate compliment.

ROOM SERVICE

4354 Lovers Lane

Dallas, TX 75225

(214) 369-7666

At Dallas's Room Service, nothing goes unused—or unnoticed—by owner Ann Fox, whose masterful ways with architectural ornaments are well known. Ann sprinkles gingerbread, latticework, porch doors, and Palladian window frames throughout her home furnishings shop to prove the value of mixing old and new for impact and effect.

ROOM WITH A VIEW

1600 Montana Avenue

Santa Monica, CA 90403

(310) 998-5858   info@roomview.com   www.roomview.com

Although aptly named, this Santa Monica home furnishings

and linens store could do with a few extra S's. There are several
rooms with several views, all of it enchanting and inviting. Owners
Elizabeth and Tom Alesio are constantly finding new designs to add
to the outstanding mix.

ROSA RUGOSA

10 Straight Wharf

Nantucket, MA 02554

(508) 228-5597

 Named for the native pink blooms that dot Nantucket Island,
Rosa Rugosa overflows with furniture hand painted in floral motifs,
unusual antiques, vintage chintzes, framed flower prints, and nauti-
cal keepsakes. With its mix of land and sea motifs, the shop is
uniquely Nantucket.

SIMPLY SANTA FE

72 East San Francisco Street

Santa Fe, NM 87501

(505) 988-3100 simplysf@roadrunner.com

 Located in a restored building on Santa Fe's historic Plaza,
Simply Santa Fe is a shop filled with luxuries large and small. From
this old storefront, stylish pieces that reflect the sophisticated tastes
of the area are bought and sold. Talented craftspeople are the back-
bone of the store, filling the dramatic space with furniture,
clothing, and home accessories that are the trademarks of the
Southwest.

TANCREDI AND MORGEN

7174 Carmel Valley Road

Carmel, CA 93923

(831) 625-4477

Sharing their work as well as their lives, Marsha and Roger Alldis combine talents and interests at Tancredi and Morgen in Carmel, California. Marsha supplies the dried wreaths, embroidered clothes, and vintage fabrics; Roger finds the pine antiques and local crafts. Together, they fill their whitewashed barn with the best of the above.

Lace

BEARLACE COTTAGE

P.O. Box 702

Park City, UT 84060

(435) 649-8804   bcrane@ditell.com

Anita Crane has spent a lifetime gathering lacy treasures, transforming them into blouses, christening gowns, bridal veils, and more. Taking a snippet here and there, Anita lovingly crafts new creations from old, worn tablecloths and trims.

HERITAGE LACE

(800) 354-0668

This lace catalog draws on the traditions of Dutch and Belgian lace for its reproduction patterns and styles, showing how versatile lace can be, whether used as a table accessory or a window treatment.

LINEN LACE

4 Lafayette Street

Washington, MO 63090

(800) 332-LACE

Owner Sunny van Nice started her lace business after traveling to Great Britain and seeing the fine lace available that wasn't being sold in the United States. Her yardages are suitable for many different uses, from pillows and place mats to sheers and shades.

LONDON LACE

215 Newbury Street

Boston, MA 02116

(800) 926-LACE   www.londonlace.com

From a town house on Boston's famous Newbury Street, Diane Loesch-Jones sells yards and panels of lace for stitching into drapes, tablecloths, valances, and more. Many of her designs are reproduced from old-world European patterns.

PAT KERR, INC.

200 Wagner Place

Memphis, TN 38103

(901) 525-5223   patkerrinc@aol.com

Couturiere Pat Kerr uses lace embellishments as a stylish signature on the clothing she designs from her Memphis studio. Pat's collection of lace includes examples from many different eras and genres, all lovingly used to trim bridal and christening gowns.

RUE DE FRANCE

78 Thames Street

Newport, RI 02840

(800) 777-0998   www.ruedefrance.com

Specializing in the charming lace curtains and panels so often seen and admired in the French countryside, Pamela Kelley has built a business importing these and other lace designs to the United States. Her catalog also carries French tablewares and fabrics.

TROUVAILLE FRANÇAISE

552 East Eighty-seventh Street

New York, NY 10128

(212) 737-6015 (by appointment only)   mbclarke@earthlink.net

By amassing an extensive collection of exquisite linens and lace through the years, Muriel Clarke has built a business specializing in finely crafted and decorated textiles. Many of her pieces are from Europe, especially France, where great pride was always taken in handmade table and bed linens.

Lighting

CHARLOTTE SMITH LAMPSHADES

4 Broadway

Valhalla, NY 10595

(914) 946-5703

Casting a warm glow on beds, tables, and desks, Charlotte Smith's lamp shades create mood and ambience from playful patterns that come alive with just a little bit of light shining through.

JOYCE AMES

(212) 799-8995 (by appointment only)

One-of-a-kind lamp shades crafted by hand from old-fashioned fabrics fill the Joyce Ames Studio. This tiny workshop is alight with activity and the warm glow of vintage textiles lovingly stitched to lamp shade frames.

NANCY GOUBRAN HOME ACCENTS

424 Kelton Avenue

Los Angeles, CA 90024

(310) 209-0110   pacificoaks@worldnet.att.net

Decoupaged shades and antiqued lamp bases make perfect partners, casting soft, lovely light on tabletops, reading chairs, desks—almost every corner of a room. In the hands of capable artists and designers, the lamps are especially enlightening—and illuminating.

SHANDELL

9 Water Street

Amesbury, MA 01913

(888) 701-8696

With a wonderful selection of nineteenth-century wallpapers at hand, Susan Schneider crafts one-of-a-kind lamp shades that emit muted color and natural light through vintage paper patterns.

ULLA DARNI

Route 23, Box 6545

Acra, NY 12405

(518) 622-3566   ullad@aol.com   www.ulladarni.com

As a lesson in soft lighting, Ulla Darni paints frosted glass lamp shades by hand for a look that has everything coming up roses. Her flower-trimmed shades—no two are ever alike—are painted on the inside of the glass to cast a romantic glow on tables, desks, and beds. Her studio is open to customers and visitors alike.

Linens

ANICHINI LA COLLEZIONE

466 North Robertson Boulevard

Los Angeles, CA 90048

(888) 230-5388

or (800) 553-5309 for additional retail information

sdollenmaier@anichini.com

Partners Patrizia Anichini and Susan Dollenmaier got their start selling antique linens in New York City to savvy collectors who understood the value of beautiful handmade things. Now they design their own line of luxurious imported linens for bed, bath, kitchen, dining room, and nursery.

D. PORTHAULT

18 East Sixty-ninth Street

New York, NY 10021

(212) 688-1660

Luxurious linens are a three-hundred-year-old tradition at
D. Porthault, where hand-embroidered monograms are still applied
to sheets, pillowcases, and napkins. This renowned house of linens
is synonymous with quality workmanship of the past and present,
produced in France and known the world over.

GARNET HILL, INC.

231 Main Street

Franconia, NH 03580

(800) 622-6216

Known for comfortable, easy-care towels and bedding, the
Garnet Hill mail-order catalog features designs that are both affordable and fashionable. The home accessories include flannels, terries,
and other favorite fabrics.

LEGACY LINENS

4730 Poplar Avenue

Memphis, TN 38117

(901) 682-6429   leglin1@aol.com

Even if you didn't inherit a trunkful of fine family linens, it's
never too late to create new bed and bath traditions with beautiful
bedding, napkins, and doilies. Lynn Murff, owner of Legacy Linens

in Memphis, does her best to prove the point by filling her shop with a lovely assortment of fabric heirlooms.

....

MILADY'S MERCANTILE

17 South Main Street

Middleborough, MA 02346

(508) 946-2121

One of the joys of owning vintage linens and laces is making them part of your everyday life, as they were meant to be. Marsha Manchester, owner of Milady's Mercantile, leads a life surrounded by napkins, table mats, doilies, coasters, and table runners, and she encourages others to do the same by introducing them to the pleasures of household linens.

....

NANCY KOLTES FINE LINENS

900 Broadway

New York, NY 10003

(212) 995-9050

fax: (212) 979-5367   nkoltes@aol.com

Nancy Koltes designs luxurious linens with a simple aesthetic in mind: The bedroom should be a soothing place, a place for respite and repose. Her sheets and pillowcases meet that end by transforming beds into places of quiet beauty that calm the spirit.

....

PALAIS ROYAL

(800) 322-3911   linens@palais.com   www.palaisroyal.com

Producing affordable table, bed, and bath linens featuring the quality and craftsmanship of the past is the goal at Palais Royal, where designs are created and then sold to retail shops around the country.

PAULA GINS ANTIQUE LINENS

7233 South Sundown Circle
Littleton, CO 80120
(303) 734-9095

Tales of beautiful antique textiles are always unfolding when dealer Paula Gins opens the door to her linen closet. Paula buys and sells vintage bed linens, christening gowns, tray cloths, nightgowns, handkerchiefs, and pillows of superb quality, sharing them with others whose passion is collecting fine linens.

PEACOCK ALLEY

(800) 810-0708

When Mary Ella Gabler perceived a void in the luxury linen market twenty-five years ago, she proceeded to fill the gap— and beautifully. Her bedding, coverlets, and pillows are a pleasure to look at and own, adding a touch of class and personality to bedrooms and baths.

SCHWEITZER LINENS

457 Columbus Avenue

New York, NY 10024

(800) L LINENS or (212) 249-8361

As a family business that grew out of old-world traditions when craftsmanship and quality were paramount, Schweitzer Linens maintains a commitment to elegant, luxurious linens for bed, bath, and table.

WHITE LINEN, INC.

520 Bedford Road

Pleasantville, NY 10570

(800) 828-0269

Devoted to reproducing the texture and filigree of the past through beautiful fabrics, Alena Gerli started White Linen, a business that is an apt expression of Alena's love of linens. Tablecloths, napkins, place mats, pillows, and duvet covers are worked in many lacy techniques—cutwork, crewel, crochet, and embroidery—to re-create an unmistakably vintage look.

Pillows

CHELSEA TEXTILES

979 Third Avenue, Suite 914

New York, NY 10022

(212) 319-5804   www.chelseatextiles.com

After studying fine examples of antique textiles from America and Europe, designers at Chelsea Textiles reproduce them using yarns and fabrics that honor the originals. In classic patterns and colors, these pillows do the past proud.

....

KATHA DIDDEL

345 Sayette Avenue

Mamaroneck, NY 10543

(914) 381-0446

Taking tapestries, embroideries, and other rich fabrics as inspiration, this company creates plush pillows that draw attention—and compliments—to a room. Versatile palettes and patterns make them suitable in a variety of settings.

....

PILLOWMAKER

(800) 611-7522 or (212) 860-8858

Pillow talk comes naturally to Kathe Williams, creator of pillows using leftover scraps of designer fabrics—tapestry, chintz, damask—that are at home on sofas, chairs, and beds. Made of fine fabrics in a well-tailored style, Kathe's pillows are comfortable additions to favorite furniture pieces.

....

VICTORY PILLOWS

P.O. Box 193, Lenox Hill Station

New York, NY 10021

(212) 688-2562

Carefully cut, pieced, and stitched from vintage textiles, these one-of-a-kind accessories make a beautiful addition—and statement—to any room. Each pillow is designed to make best use of lovely old fabrics that are worn in some places but in pristine condition in others.

$\mathcal{Q}$uilts

JEN JONES WELSH QUILTS AND BLANKETS

Pontbrendu, Llanybydder

Ceredigion, Wales SA40 9UJ England

(011) 44 1570 480610 fax: (011) 44 1570 480112

The beautifully stitched, whole-cloth quilts of Wales have long been recognized as native glories by collector Jen Jones. Jen travels the Welsh countryside in search of these wool-filled quilts and covers, most of them made between the 1870s and 1920s.

JUDI BOISSON

134 Mariner Drive

Southampton, NY 11968

(516) 283-5466   jboisson@aol.com   www.judiboisson.com

Dress a bed in one of Judi Boisson's hand-stitched quilts, and it instantly becomes the focal point of a room. Judi's designs are based on traditional quilt patterns but updated in easy-care fabrics and wide-ranging colors. Designs match just about every decorating scheme, from elegant estate to comfy cottage.

LAURA FISHER

1050 Second Avenue

New York, NY 10022

(212) 838-2596

New York City antiques dealer Laura Fisher specializes in handmade quilts, finding examples that catch her fancy and adding to her collection whenever and wherever she can. She travels all over the Northeast looking for unusual quilts in excellent condition to buy, sell, and trade.

Rugs

ELIZABETH EAKINS

21 East Sixty-fifth Street

New York, NY 10021

(212) 628-1950

Every request for a hand-hooked or hand-woven rug can be met by the talented designers at Elizabeth Eakins's studio. In their talented hands, wool and cotton rugs of superior quality and coloring take shape. Each creation is custom-made to meet the customer's needs.

KARASTAN

(800) 234-1120   karastan@karastan.com   www.karastan.com

A rug or carpet can give a room its mood and manner. When looking for just the right touch to add special artistry to a room, try a Karastan carpet underfoot. Karastan makes styles to add warmth and wit to existing furnishings.

....

NEW RIVER ARTISANS

P.O. Box 1

Piney Creek, NC 28663

(336) 359-2216

No request for a custom-made rug is too unusual for New River Artisans, a North Carolina company specializing in made-to-order floor designs. The designers here work with specific paint and fabric swatches to create wonderful wool works for the floor.

....

SIGN OF THE HOOK

21600 Davis Mill Road

Germantown, MD 20876

(301) 977-1242

Mary Sheppard Burton's hooked rugs are both decorative and utilitarian. Drawing inspiration from nature, Mary's designs tell of her love of the great outdoors with a palette of wool yarns ranging from vivid to subtle color.

....

WOODARD & GREENSTEIN

506 East Seventy-fourth Street

New York, NY 10021

(212) 794-9404   wgantiques@ad.com

From their clean, spare New York City store, collectors Thomas Woodard and Blanche Greenstein display outstanding examples of

American antiques. The owners have become especially well known for their area rugs, both old and reproduction. A large selection of hooked and woven beauties is available in varying sizes, patterns, and styles.

Stationers/Desk Accessories

ANNA GRIFFIN INVITATION DESIGN
(404) 817-8170   www.annagriffin.com

Enhancing her stationery with details usually found only on custom designs—gatefold envelopes, vellum overlays, ribbon closures, seals—Anna Griffin, a former graphic designer, creates invitations for all sorts of events, occasions, and celebrations.

DEMPSEY CARROLL
110 East Fifty-seventh Street
New York, NY 10022
(212) 486-7526

Knowing better than to tamper with tradition, this venerable house of cards and letters is known for its elegant array of traditional styles. Monogramming and other custom services are available for personal stationery.

GIFTED LINE

(800) 5-GIFTED

Gifted collector John Grossman has compiled such a vast assemblage of paper ephemera that he has developed a business based on his wondrous assortment. The Gifted Line includes gift tags, greeting cards, wraps, and stickers, all inspired by pretty papers from the past.

KATE'S PAPERIE

561 Broadway

New York, NY 10012

(212) 941-9816

Providing anything and everything pertaining to paper, this emporiumlike store offers unusual pens, journals, desk sets, blotters, stationery, sealing wax, gift wrap, and handmade paper, all designed to make the art of letter writing a complete pleasure.

MARCEL SCHURMAN

(800) 333-6724

Art and museum reproductions appear frequently on Marcel Schurman cards and papers, with a strong selection of flower and garden images. The line is especially well known for outstanding quality in paper and printing.

MRS. JOHN L. STRONG COMPANY

699 Madison Avenue

New York, NY 10021

(212) 838-3848

Generations have listened to the advice dispensed by the stationery experts at Mrs. John L. Strong Company. When it comes to writing etiquette, this sixty-year-old firm minds its p's and q's. Their engraved papers—for wedding invitations, birth announcements, and parties—are among the finest available, custom designed with each customer in mind.

....

PAPYRUS

48 Fulham Road

Chelsea, London SW3 6HH England

(011) 44 1715 848022

or

8 Upper Borough Walls, Bath BA1 1RG England

(011) 44 1225 463418   shopping@papyrusbath.demon.co.uk

www.shopping@papyrusbath.co.uk

A fascination for fine papers prompted Lula and Michael Gibson to start Papyrus, their stationery business specializing in unusual and elegant desk accessories. Marbleized papers are a specialty as well as correspondence cards, thank-you notes, and calendars.

....

PENDRAGON, INC.

27 Prospect Street

Whitinsville, MA 01588

(508) 234-6843

fax: (508) 234-5446

In Maria Thomas's calligraphy studio, every special occasion is heralded with hand-lettered flourishes on invitations, stationery, and envelopes. As Maria explains it, an invitation is a prelude of what's to come, and Maria's invitations are too beautiful to refuse.

SMYTHSON OF BOND STREET

138 Lexington Avenue

New York, NY 10016

(800) 345-6839   smythson@aol.com

Relying on venerable designs of the past, this shop stocks leather desk accessories, stationery, invitations, and more, all in both formal and informal styles. Many of Smythson's vintage-style writing papers have survived several generations to remain suitable for today's myriad uses.

STERN

47 passage des Panoramas

Paris 75002 France

(011) 33 145 088645

One of the most venerable stationers in the world—a firm that upholds letter-writing tradition with pride—resides in France. For 170 years, customers have come to Stern for elegant engraving, fine papers, formal invitations, and the kind of personal service that is not only still available, but upheld and honored.

....

THE PRINTERY
45 West Main Street
Oyster Bay, NY 11771
(516) 922-3250

Tending a printing business his grandmother started over fifty years ago, Bill Miller has nurtured The Printery along, gradually turning the mainstay of the business from newspaper printing to stationery and papers. Using old presses, Bill achieves a fine quality on everything from announcements to invitations.

....

TWO WOMEN BOXING
3002B Commerce Street
Dallas, TX 75226
(214) 939-1626 or (214) 939-2300   www.custompres@bhc.net

Keeping a journal or commonplace book becomes a beautiful endeavor with designs from this innovative company whose nicely bound books and papers are ready and waiting to record quotes, thoughts, and observations. Boxes and desk organizers are also part of the line.

....

VICTORIAN TRADING COMPANY
(800) 718-2380

Romantic images from the past adorn the cards and stationery produced by Melissa Rolston's Victorian Trading Company. The

mail-order catalog is filled with all manner of gifts and paper goods as well as reproduction desk accessories and writing implements.

Wall Coverings

BRADBURY AND BRADBURY

P.O. Box 155

Benicia, CA 94510

(707) 746-1900

info@bradbury.com   www.bradbury.com

For anyone involved in historic restoration or for those seeking the most authentic reproductions available, look no further than the Bradbury and Bradbury wallpaper books, filled with beautifully intricate and hand-colored designs.

EISENHART

(800) 931-WALL

Wallpapers make a house a home; they create just the right mood in the bedroom, study, kitchen, or bath. Eisenhart knows how to make a personal statement in every room using wallpaper to enhance almost any space.

IMPERIAL

(800) 539-5399

Handsomely produced and printed wallpaper designs by Imperial are an easy way to create big changes in your home.

Use a few rolls to spruce up just one wall, or cover an entire
room—ceiling, too—in a favorite pattern. Papers are easy
to install and maintain.

....

SANDERSON

(201) 894-8400

Known for beautiful wallcoverings and matching fabrics,
Sanderson produces florals and more to coordinate with furniture,
linens, carpets, and curtains of all styles.

....

SCHUMACHER

(800) 332-3384

Whether inspired by period patterns or more modern motifs,
Schumacher is known for the charm and appeal of its wall coverings
and coordinated fabrics. Schumacher designs have a reputation for
quality in materials and workmanship, colors and compositions.

....

YORK

(800) 375-9675

Make a magical transformation in your home with the help of
York wall coverings. The many pattern books are filled with inven-
tive ideas, stylish designs, and creative ways to use wallpapers and
borders.

....

NATURE'S
World

Florists/Flowers

BLUE MEADOW FLOWERS

336 East Thirteenth Street

New York, NY 10003

(212) 979-8618

Best described as a flower-lover's florist, Blue Meadow creates bouquets and arrangements from a tiny storefront filled with fragrant flowers. The owners like to keep their ideas as fresh as their flowers.

CAROLINE DICKERSON
(011) 44 171 245 9599

Designing for special events, this Englishwoman enjoys working "by request only" because it gives her a chance to keep her ideas tailored to specific occasions. Her flower arrangements are created once and once only; then it's on to the next custom assignment.

....

CJ FOREST AND COMPANY
2295 Peachtree Road
Atlanta, GA 30309
(404) 352-9010

Woodland spirits reign supreme at this Atlanta flower shop, where blossoms, buds, and berries look as if they were freshly gathered from a forest. Customers are convinced that wood sprites and fairies must have a hand in the creative process.

....

CHRISTIAN TORTU
6 Carrefour de l'Odéon
Paris 75006 France
(800) 753-2038 or (011) 33 1432 60256

Innovative ideas seem to grow as easily as the flowers that fill this charming store. The essence of what a perfect Paris flower shop should be, Christian Tortu is named for its designer/owner, who sets the floral trends that so many others seem to follow.

....

FIORI OF MINNEAPOLIS

(612) 623-1153

Once a gift shop that accommodated requests for flowers on the side, Fiori has retooled its image so it is first and foremost a place for flowers. This change has been good for business—and for customers in the area who long for fresh flowers creatively arranged.

FLORALS OF WATERFORD

74 East Allendale Avenue

Saddle River, NJ 07458

(201) 327-0337

Formerly innkeepers, husband and wife Mike and Katie Bartholome returned to the family fold and the business of plants and flowers. Now they tend beds of roses instead of beds of linens, and savor the change. The shop and the flowers they oversee flourish under their careful watch.

FLOWERS OF THE MEADOW

7744 Laurel Avenue

Cincinnati, OH 45243

(513) 561-0882

Presiding over a shop filled with fresh and dried flowers seems to suit owner Karen Brandenburg. Her love of anything from the garden is apparent in the mix of accessories she adds to the flowers—fruits, herbs, pinecones, bulbs, wreaths. Her grace notes spark garden images throughout this cottage-style store.

MELONIE DE FRANCE

41 East Sixtieth Street
New York, NY 10022
(212) 935-4343

Using the most vivid field flowers found in all of France, this shop is known for its tightly clustered dried flower arrangements. These compositions of color and texture can fill baskets and pots as well as take the shape of topiary trees.

REIKO M. FLORALS

734 South Washington Street
Royal Oak, MI 48067
(248) 543-5433

Twins Kathy Takenaga and Patty Kelly lavish twice the care and attention on their stunning floral arrangements. They're known for their creative use of props, containers, and color—again, a double dose of daring design.

ROBERT ISABELL

(800) ISABELL

Flowers by Robert Isabell can be elaborate or intimate, dramatic or delicate, but mostly, they are memorable. No matter what the occasion, Robert and his team create floral accessories that transform a room—and an event.

ROLLING HILLS FLOWER MART

1763 South Elena Street

Redondo Beach, CA 90277

(310) 540-3333

Christine Gaudenti's favorite arrangements often blend fruits ("the more exotic the better") with softly petaled flowers like roses and hydrangeas. She also likes to cluster several low arrangements together, scattering kumquats, grapes, and lady apples to link the vases.

SIMPLE PLEASURES

The Forge

6 Richmond Square

Providence, RI 02906

(401) 331-4120   fax: (401) 274-0609

Impromptu bouquets that look effortless stand ready and waiting to be carried out of this flower shop by customers who know how stylish Mary Moore's designs can be. Sometimes endearing, other times whimsical, always enticing, Mary's work is the picture of personal flair.

STONE KELLY EVENTS AND FLOWERS

328 Columbus Avenue

New York, NY 10023

(212) 875-0500   stonekelly@aol.com

Large or small, grand or subtle, no request for flowers is ever too big or too small at Stone Kelly. The designers have a passionate understanding of how to enhance an event or occasion with flowers.

Fruits

AMERICAN SPOON FOODS

(800) 222-5886

Thanks to plentiful harvests of tree- and vine-ripened fruits, a once-small Michigan farm is now a national purveyor of special treats for the table. American Spoon Foods, known for its preserves, jellies, honeys, and jams, turns bountiful annual yields into the freshest possible fruit spreads and confitures.

GREIG FARM

Pitcher Lane

Red Hook, NY 12571

(914) 758-1234

On certain summer days, it seems all roads lead to Red Hook, New York, where the blueberries at Greig Farm are too plump and juicy to resist. Pickers come prepared to fill buckets and pails at this family-owned farm, complete with fields for picnicking and a market for shopping.

HURD ORCHARDS

Route 104 West and Monroe-Orleans Road

Holley, NY 14470

(716) 638-8838

Home to the Hurd family for seven generations, this thousand-acre farm grows the produce that eventually fills the Hurd Orchards larder. Apples, peaches, plums, and berries all thrive in the sandy soil typical of the Great Lakes—an ideal area for preserving the freshest of fruit flavors.

Garden Shops/Garden Designers

ALEXANDRA RANDALL GARDEN DESIGN
(516) 862-9291

With the same care she took in creating wonderful wedding flowers, Alexandra Randall has turned her talents to garden design. She loves every flower that grows and seems to know just what and where things flourish and thrive in this Long Island, New York, climate and beyond.

ATLOCK FARM
545 Weston Canal Road
Somerset, NJ 08873
(732) 356-3373

Pruned to perfection, Ken Selody's topiaries range from houseplants and herbs to flowering plants and tropicals. He takes meticulous care to ensure that his plants are carefully clipped and watered so they have a long life once they are purchased and taken home.

CONNI CROSS LANDSCAPE DESIGN

P.O. Box 730

Cutchogue, NY 11935

(516) 734-6874

Ever resourceful and knowledgeable, Conni Cross likes nothing better than digging around in the dirt. To create landscapes that are constantly new and surprising, Conni explores every path and possibility available to her.

COOKS GARDEN

P.O. Box 5010

Hodges, SC 29653

(802) 824-3400

Whether an heirloom variety or an up-to-the-minute hybrid, Cooks Garden knows its vegetables. Plants and seeds are available for lettuces, tomatoes, onions, and herbs—a true kitchen garden resource for all kinds of cooks.

ELEGANT EARTH

1301 First Avenue North

Birmingham, AL 35203-1727

(800) 242-7758 (by appointment only)

fax: (205) 324-7555

Displaying antiques in the garden is not a new idea, but no one does it as stylishly as Jane Comer at Birmingham's Elegant Earth. Using fountains, statuary, weather vanes, benches, and sundials to enhance her landscapes, Jane creates inviting outdoor places of all shapes, sizes, and scales.

....

FOXGLOVE FARM

6741 224th Street

Langley, BC V2Y 2K5 Canada

(604) 888-4140   foxglove_farm@compuserve.com

From a historic agricultural area near Vancouver, Rebecca Black grows an endless variety of field flowers. In summer, her farm features hillsides covered with flowers and awash in color. Once harvested and dried, the flowers are just right for the wreaths and arrangements she creates in her weathered old barn.

....

GARDEN MEMORIES

424 Main Street

Ventura, CA 93001

(805) 641-1070

Potpourris, herb teas, and garden books happily coexist among the flowers and plants that Barbara Malmain nurtures in her California shop. On nice days, the flowers often spill outside the front door so customers can glimpse the goodies to be found within.

....

GUY WOLFF

725 Bantam Road

Bantam, CT 06750

(860) 567-7040   gwolff@javanet.com   www.guywolff.com

Who says garden planters can't be pretty and practical all in one? From Guy Wolff's able hands come hand-thrown terra-cotta pots that manage to be both fun and functional. These decorative designs have gardeners everywhere singing their praises.

NANCY MCCABE GARDEN DESIGN

P.O. Box 447

Salisbury, CT 06068

(860) 824-5728

fax: (860) 824-4690

After years of experimenting in her own backyard, Nancy McCabe knows the Connecticut climate so well, she can recommend plants and bulbs with confidence. Call her for advice on what to grow where.

PAULINE RUNKLE

(978) 526-4159

fax: (978) 526-8628   pauliner@earthlink.net

www.paulinesbouquets.com

Garden designer Pauline Runkle knows just how to coax maximum beauty from favorite flowers—peonies, roses, lilacs, sweet peas, lilies of the valley—and she graciously shares what she knows with others. While conducting garden workshops and semi-

nars, Pauline imparts knowledge gained from her years of trial
and error experiences.

....

POT LUCK STORE

23 Main Street

Accord, NY 12404

(914) 626-2300

Not long ago, when Karen Skelton was casting about for new
career opportunities, she decided to take a ceramics class. The class
proved so rewarding that Karen was certain she had found her calling. Soon after, she launched a line of garden pots, and a short time
later, she opened a store to sell her garden goods.

....

POTTED GARDENS

27 Bedford Street

New York, NY 10014

(212) 255-4797

Container gardening takes on a whole new meaning in the
capable hands of Rebecca Cole, owner of New York City's Potted
Gardens. Rebecca finds the makings for wonderful self-contained
gardens in old, cast-off china, tinware—even luggage.

....

ROMANCING THE WOODS

33 Raycliffe Drive

Woodstock, NY 12498

(914) 246-6976 davis@rtw-inc.com www.rtw-inc.com

With little more than well-hewn branches and logs in hand,

Marvin Davis creates garden gates, bridges, arbors, gazebos, and benches to enhance any outdoor setting. Along with the branches and logs that have become Marvin's trademark, he brings an expert's eye for design and detail.

....

ROSE HEDGE COTTAGE

4688 Bath Pike

Bethlehem, PA 18017-9012

(610) 865-8454

Living *la vie en rose* from her Pennsylvania property, Rita Sillivan Smith creates flower-filled landscapes for herself and others using roses as her central theme. Rita favors pretty, perfumed varieties, designing her gardens to bloom continually throughout the growing season.

....

SHEPHERD GARDEN SEEDS

30 Irene Street

Torrington, CT 06790

(860) 482-3638   www.shepherdseeds.com

Anxious to sample fresh new tastes from the garden, Renee Shepherd started experimenting with seeds she could grow in her own backyard. Before she knew it, Renee was sharing the fruits—and vegetables—of her labors with others in search of wonderful homegrown crops.

....

TERRA COTTA

11925 Montana Avenue

and 11922 San Vicente Boulevard

Los Angeles, CA 90049

(310) 826-7878   terracotta@earthlink.net

Naturals are a running theme at Terra Cotta: The fruits, flowers, even the decorative accessories all carry the look of nature's finest. The designers here work with the best that nature offers and embellish with creative ideas of their own.

TREILLAGE, LTD.

418 East Seventy-fifth Street

New York, NY 10021

(212) 535-2288   fax: (212) 517-6589

With a love of all things garden-related, Bunny Williams has created the store of her dreams. Treillage, purveyor of well-designed garden tools and accessories, is located in a former carriage house, allowing lots of display space for special objects from and for the garden.

VICTORY GARDEN

63 Main Street

East Hampton, NY 11937

(516) 324-7800

Selling to customers who love bringing the garden indoors, Paola Schulhof specializes in florals and antiques that work in both settings. Whether interested in a gloriette, a pair of urns, or framed botanicals, customers find their heart's desire.

WELL-SWEEP HERB FARM

205 Mt. Bethel Road

Port Murray, NJ 07865

(908) 852-5390

Well-Sweep Herb Farm, a quiet piece of property located in the back hills of New Jersey, is renowned for its unique collection of dried flowers and rare herbs. That's good news for gardeners who happen upon this open-for-business farm, where plants are not only for sale but also available by mail.

WHICHFORD POTTERY

Whichford Shipston-on-Stour

Warwickshire CV36 5PG England

(011) 44 1608 684 416

Potted perfection is how loyalists describe the wares of Whichford Pottery. Founded in the English Cotswolds sixteen years ago by plantsman Jim Keeling, Whichford is now an established presence in the world of gardening.

WILD CHILD

333 Main Street

Wakefield, RI 02879

(401) 782-8944   wildchild@snet.net   www.sprig.net

Everything Monica Schaffer touches seems to grow—including her business, a shop devoted to her love of nature. Monica has always carried flowers and herbs but has recently branched out into

fashion and furnishings that meet her strict standards for respecting
the environment and the natural world.

....

WILD THYME

5725 Kennett Pike

Centreville, DE 19807

(302) 656-4454

With acres of flowers just a stone's throw from her front door,
gardener Laurie de Grazia takes advantage of the opportunity presented her. She offers fresh-cut flowers—dahlias, zinnias, sunflowers—that might not be available to her customers if she hadn't sown
these unusual seeds herself.

Herbs

CAPRILANDS

Silver Street

Coventry, CT 06238

(860) 742-7244   www.caprilands.com

Founded over sixty years ago, Caprilands Herb Farm has been
lovingly tended since the time when herbs were thought of as nothing more than weeds. Now that the tide has turned and gardeners
are enamored of their many charms, herbs are bought and sold at
Caprilands for a variety of purposes—both culinary and medicinal.

....

DIAMOND ORGANICS

(800) 922-2396

Steeped in tradition and beautifully fragrant, these herbs lend a special enchantment to garden and kitchen pursuits. The herbs grown by Diamond Organics are completely natural, free of the chemicals purists hope to avoid.

....

FREDERICKSBURG HERB FARM

402 Whitney Street

Fredericksburg, TX 78624

(800) 259 HERB   herbfarm@kts.com

www.fredericksburgherbfarm.com

In the hills of Texas, Bill and Sylvia Varney have created an herbal idyll, enthusiastically sharing their romance with herbs with anyone who visits the garden, shop, and tearoom. Their knowledge of herbs runs as deep as the roots of the many plants they nurture on their farm.

....

THE HERBFARM

32804 Issaquah–Fall City Road

Fall City, WA 98024

(206) 784-2222   customerservice@theherbfarm.com

www.theherbfarm.com

During most of the year, every field is in flower at The Herb-farm, a culinary garden near Seattle where herbs are not only grown and sold but are used to create the tantalizing fare served on the premises for summer dinners and special occasions.

PECONIC RIVER HERB FARM

2749 River Road

Calverton, NY 11933

(516) 369-0058

Cris Spindler can usually be found knee deep in herbs on her Long Island farm, where the "useful plants" she grows find their way into homemade jams and teas. Cris uses herbs in all sorts of ways—some expected, some surprising, all imaginative—and encourages visitors to the farm to do the same.

RAVENHILL HERB FARM

1330 Mt. Newton X Road

Saanichton, BC V8M 1S1 Canada

(250) 652-4024   andnoel@pacificcoast.net

Extensive herb gardens just a short ferry ride from Vancouver, British Columbia, are Ravenhill Herb Farm's pride and joy. For those who find their way to this pretty, rustic setting, much pleasure is to be had seeing, learning about, and taking home plants and herbs freshly dug from the ground.

SHALE HILL FARM AND HERB GARDEN

134 Hommelville Road

Saugerties, NY 12477

(914) 246-6982

Touring the gardens at Shale Hill Farm with owner Pat Reppert is an education in herb legend and lore. Those who visit her farm and gift shop are as likely to fall under the spell of herbs as this experienced gardener.

....

SUNDANCE FARMS

3303 West 2400 South

Charleston, UT 84032

(800) 510-8667   sundancefarms@shadowlink.net

www.citysearch.com/slc/sundancefarms

    High in the mountain fields of Utah, the herbs and wildflowers at Sundance Farms thrive. Everything here is grown organically, enhancing the flavors of the herbs and the colors of the flowers. And everything grown is put to good use—for both culinary and decorative purposes.

....

SUNRISE HERB FARM

35 Codfish Hill Road

Bethel, CT 06801

(203) 794-0809

fax: (203) 792-4701   gaia188@aol.com

www.sunriseherbfarm.com

    Herbalist extraordinaire Valerie Hoffman loves the legend and lore of garden herbs, which is clear the moment visitors step onto her Connecticut farm. As a firm believer in the many valuable properties of herbs, Valerie promotes their use in cooking, crafting, and healing.

Nurseries/Plants

AÑO NUEVO FLOWER GROWERS

1701 Cabrillo Highway

Pescadero, CA 94060

(650) 879-0389

California's Garibaldi family is among the very few violet growers left in the United States. Many abandoned the trade when old-fashioned flowers went out of style in the 1980s. Now that violets have made a strong comeback, the Garibaldis are delighted to continue a family tradition that is almost a century old.

BONNY DOON FARMS

600 Martin Road

Santa Cruz, CA 95060

(831) 459-0967   fax: (831) 459-6700

From her farm near the California coast in the Santa Cruz Mountains, Diane Meehan cultivates a wide range of herbs and flowers, including several fragrant varieties of lavender. The sunny climate is ideal for the bountiful crop at Bonny Doon Farm, harvested by hand and used a variety of ways, both fresh and dried.

CIDER HILL GARDEN

1747 Hunt Road

Windsor, VT 05089

(802) 674-5293   milecart@sovernet.com

In the gardens and greenhouses of Vermont's Cider Hill Farm, there's always a new herb to discover, a gardening tip to dispense, an idea whose time has come. Owners Sarah and Gary Milek revel in the joys of crafting and cooking with plants and herbs, sharing their joy with those who visit the garden.

....

PRAIRIE NURSERY

P.O. Box 306

Westfield, WI 53964

(608) 296-3679 www.prairienursery.com

Flowers stretch as far as the eye can see at Prairie Nursery, where the star attraction is American wildflowers. These native plants have grown in American soil for ages, but ever since 1972 when the nursery was founded, they have truly flourished thanks to the efforts of owner Neil Diboll.

....

QUAIL RUN FARM

32200 Quail Run, P.O. Box 257

Tangent, OR 97389

(541) 928-7739

When the fields are thick with purple and the air is steeped in the sharp, clean scent of lavender, the Hagertys are ready for another harvest on their Oregon farm. Although unusual in this part of the country, the lavender crop at this family farm is both beautiful and bountiful.

....

WAYSIDE GARDENS

(800) 845-1124

The fine-quality mail-order plants available at Wayside Gardens make this catalog one of the most valued in the country. From hostas to hydrangeas, foxgloves to fuchsias, delphiniums to dahlias, this South Carolina grower has the garden market well covered. The rose selection alone offers hundreds of choices.

YERBA BUENA NURSERY

Skyline Boulevard

Woodside, CA 94062

(650) 851-1668   www.yerbabuenanursery.com

When plant lovers come upon a hillside garden thick with California flora, they know they've reached their desired destination. Yerba Buena Nursery calls gardeners from far and wide to soak up the beauty that has been cultivated here for half a century—in greenhouses, potting sheds, lathe houses, and every fertile patch of ground.

Potpourri

ANGELA FLANDERS

96 Columbia Road

London E27 QB England

(011) 44 171 739 7555

Angela Flanders's potpourris are like bouquets scattered by a breeze, an appealing tumble of open petals and curled buds, burnished pods and fragrant fruits. Her blends are every bit as luscious to the eye as to the nose, captivating all the senses with just one whiff—or glance.

AROMATIQUE

(800) 875-3111

Patti Upton lives her life surrounded by scent—as might be expected of a designer of decorative fragrances. Her home and her office are filled with the candles, petals, and potpourris of her trade, all marketed under the Aromatique name.

CHERCHEZ

P.O. Box 550

Millbrook, NY 12545

(800) 422-1744

"I have always felt that one's home should smell as beautiful as it looks," says Barbara Ohrbach, creator of Cherchez potpourri. To that end, Barbara has devoted many hours in the garden developing unique blends that invite the outdoors in. Her fragrances mix floral, spicy, and herbal notes in appealing ways.

Roses

ANTIQUE ROSE EMPORIUM

9300 Luechemeyer Road

Brenham, TX 77833

(800) 441-0002

Michael Shoup is the first to admit that he is on a mission to

save forgotten roses. His mission began over fifteen years ago and continues today from an eight-acre Texas garden that provides safe haven for "lost" varieties. These old-fashioned flowers are nurtured by Michael, a former landscape designer, who preserves these garden heirlooms with gusto.

DAVID AUSTIN ROSES, LTD.

Bowling Green Lane
Albrighton, Wolverhampton WV7 3HB England
(011) 44 19023 73931

Offering one of the largest selections of old roses anywhere, English nurseryman David Austin also hybridizes his own, combining the delicacy and fragrance of antique roses with a broad color range and repeated blooming season. These are "new roses in the old tradition," says David, who gives equal importance to beauty and scent in the flowers he breeds.

GLEBE HOUSE

P.O. Box 245
Hollow Road
Woodbury, CT 06789
(203) 263-2855   ghmgjg@wtcl.net

In Woodbury, Connecticut, stands the only existing garden in America planned by renowned English horticultural designer Gertrude Jekyll. From May on, Glebe House garden is a spectacular vision of old-fashioned flowers, the very ones Gertrude loved to use in her landscapes, including roses galore.

JUNGLE ROSES

(800) 737-7328

Grown in the misty rain forest of South America, these large-petaled roses open into lush, fragrant blooms. Specially devised and developed to help recultivate the rain forest's depleted land, the fresh roses are shipped cross-country from the company headquarters in California.

PLANTING FIELDS

P.O. Box 58

Oyster Bay, NY 11771

(516) 922-9201

Once a private estate, Long Island's Planting Fields is now part of the New York State park system. Roses, a favorite of former owners William and Mai Coe, still grace the gardens, along with azaleas, rhododendrons, and camellias.

ROYALL RIVER ROSES

(800) 820-5830   roses@royallriverroses.com   www.royallriverroses.com

At this organic nursery in Maine, it's possible to re-create the splendor of your grandmother's garden with both antique heirloom roses and glorious new varieties, available on site or from an impressive mail-order catalog.

Beautiful
WEARABLES

Fashion

ANNE FONTAINE

318 Boylston Street

Boston, MA 02116

(617) 423-0366

or 5450 West Lovers Lane, #131 Dallas, TX 75209

(214) 956-0800   www.annefontaine.com

Beautiful blouses by Anne Fontaine are stylishly elegant on occasions that call for that single fashion accent to turn a pair of pants or a skirt into an outfit suitable for an enchanted evening.

ANN VUILLE

140 Water Street

Norwalk, CT 06854

(203) 853-2251 ava@connix.com

Adorned with silk flowers, taffeta bows, and satin ribbons, these hair ornaments and hats look like they came from a flower shop, not a design studio. "I try to choose combinations that mimic nature," explains Ann Vuille, creator of these fashion whimsies.

BARBOUR

Meadowbrook Drive

Milford, NH 03055

(800) 338-3474 www.barbour.com

The Brits know best how to deal with London fog and rain: They bring out their brollies and Barbours. In inclement weather, waterproof coats bearing the name of Victorian haberdasher John Barbour are the favored garb of the sporting set.

CORNELIA POWELL

271B East Paces Ferry Road

Atlanta, GA 30305

(404) 365-8511 www.corneliapowell.com

Taking pride in beautiful fabrics and the perfect fit, Cornelia Powell fills her Atlanta shop with dresses and blouses imaginatively restyled using vintage fabrics. Cornelia creates custom designs for customers who love the look of old with contemporary cut and flair.

CYNTHIA ROWLEY

112 Wooster Street

New York, NY 10012

(212) 334-1144

With sweater, skirt, and dress designs as fresh as a daisy, it's no wonder Cynthia Rowley has become America's fashion sweetheart. Her styles are both modern and feminine, but never trendy. Often retro-inspired, Rowley originals are more comfortable than their old-fashioned counterparts—and the fit follows the contours of today's silhouettes.

DULKEN AND DERRICK

12 West Twenty-first Street

New York, NY 10010

(212) 929-3614   topsilks@aol.com

From the hands of Lisa Dulken and Pamela Gurock, exquisite flowers are crafted of the finest silk and velvet to adorn jacket lapels, pretty lace blouses, and broad-brimmed hats. Using old-world techniques and materials, Lisa and Pamela create fanciful fabric flowers for couturiers and milliners the world over.

ELIZABETH GILLETT

237 West Thirty-fifth Street

New York, NY 10001

(212) 629-7993

Beautifully designed scarves, wraps, shawls, and shrugs are Elizabeth Gillett's stock-in-trade. Be they beaded or pleated, silk or sequined, these creations are so versatile, they work a variety of different ways to expand and embellish all kinds of wardrobes.

....

FILIGREE

1156 Yonge Street

Toronto, Ontario M4W 2L9 Canada

(416) 961-5223

Fancy filigree can embellish anything from art to architecture. At this Toronto store it aptly describes the graceful clothes that hang like lacy clouds from armoires, racks, and hooks. Shoppers also find jewelry, hatboxes, and other fashion accessories in this lovely mélange.

....

GORSUCH

(800) 525-9808

It took two former Olympic skiers to design the kind of clothes that combine the warmth, comfort, and style skiers and other outdoor enthusiasts really want and need. From Vail, Colorado—and in their mail-order catalog—Renie and David Gorsuch share alpine-inspired clothes with those who want to look cool while staying warm.

....

KATY KANE

34 West Ferry Street

New Hope, PA 18938

(215) 862-5873

Look into Katy Kane's for clothing from the past that is slightly altered to look entirely new. And while there, don't miss the vintage linens that carry a hint of the past—doilies, coasters, hand towels, and dresser scarves.

....

KEVIN SIMON CLOTHING

1358 Abbot Kinney Boulevard

Venice, CA 90291

(310) 827-6710   kevinsimon@aol.com

Since her mother is a tailor, it's not surprising that Kevin Simon grew up surrounded by—and loving—dressmaker forms, sewing machines, and all the accoutrements of the needle arts. When she started designing on her own, her whole family pitched in to launch Kevin's own line of clothing from her California studio.

....

LEGACY

109 Thompson Street

New York, NY 10012

(212) 966-4827

Is it vintage or is it now? According to shop owner Rita Brookoff, it's all the same thing. Customers who shop at Legacy expect to find traditional styling from the past gracing the thoroughly contemporary clothes found here.

....

MATSU

259 Newbury Street

Boston, MA 02116

(617) 266-9707

A cozy mix of fashions and furnishings turn this delightful shop

into a place to linger. Customers find cloches on hat stands, handbags on hangers, sweaters in drawers, and dresses on pegs—all arranged in charming vignettes.

....

N. PEAL CASHMERE

5 West Fifty-sixth Street

New York, NY 10019

(212) 333-3500

Come to N. Peal for the softest cashmere to be found. Casual separates—sweaters, coats, trousers, and scarves—are fashioned from this luxurious fabric (imported from Scotland and Italy) to comprise each season's collection. Look for updated classics like twin sets and capes.

....

OILILY

820 Madison Avenue

New York, NY 10021

(212) 772-8686

or (800) 977-7736 for retail information

With a kaleidoscope of color and a patchwork of patterns, clothes by Oilily instantly spruce up any wardrobe, adding a stylish touch to all sorts of accessories. Specializing in sweaters, jackets, skirts, and dresses, Oilily designs for children as well as women.

....

PARIS 1900

2703 Main Street

Santa Monica, CA 90405

(310) 396-0405

Enchantment reigns at Paris 1900, a Santa Monica shop with a memorable medley of vintage clothing for women and girls. Summery white cottons are a specialty here, and with a few snips and tucks, these durable, easy-care clothes are still remarkably stylish.

REFLECTIONS OF THE PAST ANTIQUE FASHIONS AND TEXTILES

P.O. Box 40361

Bay Village, OH 44140

(440) 835-6924   www.victoriana.com/antiques

Dating from the eighteenth century, Joanne Haug's fashions and textiles make an awesome impression. To make these treasured fabric finds available to a wider audience, Joanne has developed a website featuring linens, towels, and clothing from another era.

WOODLAND WADERS

P.O. Box 1774

Vineyard Haven, MA 02568

(508) 693-1598   www.vineyard.net/biz/woodland

Knowing firsthand of the need for warm, comfortable women's wear with sophisticated styling, designer Valerie Beggs creates clothes just right for hiking and other outdoor activities. Valerie's love of the outdoors works beautifully with her desire to clothe "the contemporary woodswoman."

Jewelers/Jewelry

BROKEN CHINA BY LINDA CARRIGAN

1298 Panther Hollow Drive

Bandera, TX 78003-5912

(830) 460-3373   www.BrokenChinaJewelry.com

Never discard, always reuse is Linda Carrigan's motto as she picks her way through pieces of broken china to create lovely brooches, bracelets, and pendants. Her jewelry designs make maximum use of the pretty patterns found on porcelain plates and chipped china of all kinds.

CAMILLA DIETZ BERGERON, LTD.

818 Madison Avenue

New York, NY 10021

(212) 794-9100 (by appointment only)

Those passionate about fine jewelry will find their heart's desire when they schedule an appointment to view Camilla Dietz Bergeron's collection. Her pieces, both unique and antique, are of the finest quality and represent a wide range of styles.

FACES OF TIME

32 West Fortieth Street

New York, NY 10018

(212) 921-0822   fax: (212) 719-3111

or 8 Bishop Lane, Madison, CT 06443

(203) 245-2775   fax: (203) 245-4501

Since there's nothing new under the sun fashionwise, Faces of Time takes the best of the past and rework it into stunning jewelry for today. The watches, pins, earrings, and bracelets carry a bit of nostalgia but are firmly anchored to the styles of today.

FORGET-ME-NOTS

1715 East Lamar Boulevard

Arlington, TX 76006

(817) 861-4747

Hearts by the dozens adorn the charm bracelets and necklaces that are Joan Ross's specialty. Some are antiques, others reproductions—and when assembled on one of the many silver chains she carries in her shop, all are irresistible.

JAMIE KOLE

27 Madison Avenue

Maplewood, NJ 07040

(973) 763-4926

Jewelry devotees eagerly seek out Jamie Kole's new designs as soon as they become available. Her unusual pieces are glittering col-

lages of little stones and ribbons under glass—endearing creations
that become both meaningful and collectible.

....

J. MAVEC & COMPANY, LTD.

946 Madison Avenue

New York, NY 10021

(212) 517-7665

For stickpins, earrings, cameos, watches, and other elegant heirloom designs, the J. Mavec & Company store is a jewelry lover's
dream come true. Shop to your heart's content for period designs
(especially late Victorian, Edwardian, Georgian) in a variety of
gems, metals, and other materials.

....

KARA GAFFNEY

(212) 317-9000 (by appointment only)

"I've loved jewelry since I was a little girl," says Kara Gaffney,
and after viewing her wares, one can see Kara comes to jewelry
making quite naturally. After studying gemology, Kara was ready to
launch a line of her own—with work that is handsome yet feminine
all at once.

....

MARLENE HARRIS COLLECTION

238½ Freeport Road

Pittsburg, PA 15238

(412) 828-1245   marharco@sgi.net

This savvy collector has a sixth sense when it comes to finding
antique and estate jewelry and finely crafted accessories. From

her jewel box of a shop, Marlene shares her treasures with customers seeking garnet earrings, porcelain hat pins, bejeweled ladies watches, feminine-style cuff links, elegant wedding bands, and rings of all shapes and sizes.

SAGE

311 North Martel Street

Los Angeles, CA 90036

(323) 938-0402

Sage produces wonderfully wearable jewelry with an outstanding eye for fine design and an appreciation of how rings, bracelets, and brooches can turn an outfit into a true ensemble.

SEIDENGANG

14 Elm Place

Rye, NY 10580

(800) 227-4890 or (914) 925-0788

The best jewelry is not only beautiful but practical, claim Carol Seiden and Carolyn Gang, who give their pretty designs purpose: lockets hold photos, bracelets have watch faces, beads become cuff links.

TERRY RODGERS & MELODY

1050 Second Avenue

New York, NY 10022

(212) 758-3164

This mother-daughter duo is known for their vast collection of vintage jewelry. The pieces range from Art Deco to Edwardian, from Georgian to Victorian—all one-of-a-kind and all antique. Jewelry afficionados will find earrings, cameos, bracelets, brooches, necklaces, and hair ornaments in many price ranges from this reputable store.

WELLS-WARE

P.O. Box 1596

New York, NY 10025

(888) 90 WELLS or (212) 222-9177

Designing jewelry using personal trinkets and tokens, Wells Jenkins is an archivist of sorts. She works with old photos, snippets of lace, antique watch faces, mother-of-pearl buttons, and other keepsakes from the past to fashion necklaces, bracelets, pins, earrings, and cuff links.

Lingerie

EILEEN WEST

525 Brannan Street, #300

San Francisco, CA 94107

(415) 957-9378

At-home wear that looks as good the next morning as it did the night before—this is the fashion niche Eileen West knows best. These luxurious designs make the transition from evening hours to morning with comfort and style.

FROU-FROU DESIGNS

301318 Homer Street

Vancouver, BC V6B 2V3 Canada

(604) 682-5536

fax: (604) 682-5541   froufrou@mdi.ca

Designed in all sizes with an eye for comfort and style, Frou-Frou's at-home fashions promise robes, pajamas, and sleepwear the whole family will love. Cottons, flannels, and other natural fabrics are the hands-down favorites here.

NANCY MEYER

1318 Fifth Avenue

Seattle, WA 98101

(206) 625-9200   fax: (206) 625-9281

Women in search of intimate apparel know that a visit to Nancy Meyer in Seattle is almost as good as a trip to Europe. Customers find luxurious lingerie by the best European designers here—with an ample sprinkling of young American up-and-comers added in.

....

NOCTURNE

698 Madison Avenue

New York, NY 10021

(800) 229-2607 or (212) 750-2951

With many followers and much experience, Nocturne occupies a distinguished position in the lingerie market. These lovely wares appeal to many buyers, especially those who love a lace-trimmed robe, an embroidered nightgown, and other comfy cotton sleepwear.

Milliners

....

EDNA MAE'S MILLINERY

174 Bellevue Avenue, #314

Newport, RI 02840

(401) 847-8665

Velvet, silk, netting, ribbon, chenille—with makings like these, it's no wonder Jamie Kurtis's hat creations are sought after by brides, mothers of brides, and anyone who enjoys donning a stylish hat for a special occasion.

....

FINO FINO

75 Arbor Road

Menlo Park, CA 94025

(650) 321-8720   finehats@finofino.com   www.finofino.com

—For those on the straw hat circuit, California's Fino Fino is an essential stop. Owner Carolyn Busch, also known as the glad hatter, not only sells stylish straws but also advises customers on how, where, and when to wear their new accessories.

....

HEARTFELT BY JAN STANTON

200 South Cliffwood Avenue

Los Angeles, CA 90049

(310) 393-6916

fax: (310) 393-0928   www.hatsny.com

Produced with the help of expert milliners here and abroad, designer Jan Stanton's hats are hand blocked, lined, and embellished with ribbons, flowers, and buttons. She is especially well known for her 1920s-style cloches that hug the head in a flattering fit.

....

LOUISE GREEN

1616 Cotner Avenue

Los Angeles, CA 90025

(310) 393-8231

These hats, known for attention to detail, beautiful embellishment, and unusual ornamentation, are eye-catching but subtle. The designs are definite fashion statements, yet work as accessories for many different outfits.

PATRICIA UNDERWOOD

498 Seventh Avenue, 24th Floor

New York, NY 10018

(212) 268-3774   hatunderwood@earthlink.net

All of the hats produced by this respected designer carry an elegance that is unmistakably Underwood. Patricia's styles are so well crafted they need almost no adornment. Her straws range from simple to glamorous, low profile to high drama.

PAUL'S HAT WORKS

6128 Geary Boulevard

San Francisco, CA 94121

(415) 221-5332

Owner Michael Harris is quick to share his knowledge of authentic panama straw hats—fedoras, planters, optimos—with customers who visit his San Francisco shop. Once you decide on a style, he measures your head for a perfect fit, then hand-finishes each one with 1940s grosgrain ribbons.

PETER BEATON HATS

16½ Federal Street

Nantucket, MA 02554

(508) 228-8684

An island setting seems ideally suited to the straw styles designed by Darcy Creech for Peter Beaton Hats. Her hats are as fresh as the ocean breezes that blow down Nantucket's main shopping street, which is where you'll find Darcy's designs being sold in a wonderful old storefront.

....

VAN DER LINDE DESIGNS

11 East Fifty-sixth Street

New York, NY 10022

(212) 758-1686 (by appointment only)

Brimming with good spirit, hats by Van der Linde Designs are so versatile and uplifting, you'll want to wear them everywhere. Especially popular are the fabric and straw styles.

Shoes

....

AMY JO GLADSTONE

44-02 Eleventh Street

Long Island City, NY 11101

(718) 706-0300

fax: (718) 706-7878

Without surrendering style to comfort, Amy Jo Gladstone designs slippers that are worthy of Cinderella. Her line consists of styles that keep feet content while managing to be attractive accessories you're proud to wear.

....

MARK SCHWARTZ AT ABOUT TIME

15 Prince Street

New York, NY 10012

(212) 941-0966

Fine materials and good design are two constant components of couture shoes by Mark Schwartz. These styles perfectly complement today's tastes—from long, flowing skirts to tailored pants.

VANESSA NOEL

12 West Fifty-seventh Street, #901

New York, NY 10019

(212) 333-7882

Anyone who steps out in a pair of Vanessa Noel pumps knows no shoe is prettier—or better made. These distinctive styles include some made of silk or satin, some trimmed with antique buckles, and others embellished with hand-sewn rosettes.

YONA LEVINE

59 East Third Street

New York, NY 10003

(212) 777-5260

Designer Yona Levine does some fancy footwork to create fashionable shoes for brides, debs—anyone who understands and appreciates the appeal of well-dressed feet. Some of Yona's styles rely on fine upholstery fabrics, others are crafted of soft cotton. Her signature mules use supple straw as a main material.

Wedding Gowns/Veils

AMSALE BRIDAL BOUTIQUE

625 Madison Avenue

New York, NY 10022

(212) 583-1700 or (800) 765-0170 for retail information

Artful ensembles from Amsale make every bride feel she's wearing a one-of-a-kind dress that is hers and hers alone. Custom fittings enhance the experience—and the allure.

HELEN MORLEY

226 West Thirty-seventh Street, #401

New York, NY 10018

(212) 594-6404   fax: (212) 268-5442

info@helenmorley.com   www.helenmorley.com

"The most important point about a wedding gown is how it fits," says English-born designer Helen Morley, who also takes great care with design and detail once the fit is just so. When a bride steps into one of these dazzling dresses, all she needs is an aisle and a smile.

JANA STARR ANTIQUES

236 East Eightieth Street

New York, NY 10021

(212) 861-8256

Jana, who started out as an antiques dealer but gravitated toward bridal clothing and linens, restores and alters vintage dresses, veils, headpieces, and more, giving modern weddings a stylish "something old."

JESSICA MCCLINTOCK

(800) 711-8718

Time and time again, fashionable women look to Jessica McClintock for the romantic yet sophisticated clothes they want to wear. Her wedding dresses, too, provide the subtle adornments and endearing qualities brides love—lacy accents, embroidered details, elegant trims.

PRISCILLA OF BOSTON

137 Newbury Street

Boston, MA 02116

(617) 267-9070   www.priscillaofboston.com

With a shimmer of satin, a sweep of organza, a length of lace netting, this venerable fashion house styles wedding gowns, each one carrying the elegant signature of its creator Priscilla Kidder.

REBECCA LEWIS HOUSE OF DESIGN

(800) 301-8933 or (617) 261-9922

hod@hod.com   www.hod.com

Every bride hopes that her wedding attire looks custom-made especially for her. That's the secret behind Rebecca Lewis's bridal designs. These gowns create their own style depending on who wears them and how.

TIA MAZZA

(212) 989-4349

fax: (212) 924-4121

Creating headpieces as special as the day itself, Tia Mazza outfits brides in the accessories of their dreams using a wonderful array of fabrics and trims. If a bride looks beautiful from top to toe, Tia can certainly take credit for the "top."

ULLA-MAIJA

24 West Fortieth Street

New York, NY 10018

(212) 768-0707

fax: (212) 768-4609

Designing an elegant bridal collection that reflects her love of flowers and fashion, Ulla-Maija works wonders with luxurious fabrics and stylish trims. Her gowns are known for their flattering fit, masterfully made to suit the silhouette of each customer.

VERA WANG

991 Madison Avenue

New York, NY 10021

(212) 628-3400

The gowns of Vera Wang are part ballerina, part princess—a winning combination for any bride who's ever wanted to be part of a fairy-tale wedding and live happily ever after.

YUMI KATSURA BOUTIQUE

907 Madison Avenue

New York, NY 10021

(212) 772-3760

Dazzling dresses with impressive details and flattering lines are the strong suit at Yumi Katsura Boutique. These bridal gowns appeal to sophisticated women with a strong sense of style—women who enjoy fashion and want to express their personal style in the gown they choose to wear on their wedding day.

Personal

BEAUTY

Beauty

AESOP

(888) 223-2750

Aesop's skin care products, made in Australia, cleanse, balance, and hydrate in the purest way possible. Using plant oils and extracts, Aesop approaches the notion of beauty through the skin's well-being, treating it delicately, but seriously.

AROMAFLORIA

(800) 424-0034   www.aromafloria.com

Fans of Aromafloria cite the soothing, healing, comforting properties of the products. The bath and body products are natural, using essential oils and herbs as main ingredients. Many are designed to eliminate stress, protect the skin, and remedy problem areas.

BETTER BOTANICALS

3066 M Street NW

Washington, DC 20007

(888) BB HERBS

fax: (202) 625-6624

bbherbs@betterbotanicals.com   www.betterbotanicals.com

Packed with nutrient-rich oils and botanicals, these herbal products take a natural approach to beauty. They enhance hair and skin for a lifetime of good health and gentle care.

BOBBI BROWN

600 Madison Avenue, 18th Floor

New York, NY 10022

(212) 980-7040   www.bobbibrowncosmetics.com

As a professional makeup artist, Bobbi Brown always believed "you should notice the woman, not what she's wearing." When she developed her own line of cosmetics, she was committed to a natural palette, allowing women to find their own personal style rather than follow trends.

CASWELL-MASSEY

518 Lexington Avenue

New York, NY 10017

(212) 755-2254

The first apothecary to bring fine toiletries to American shores, Caswell-Massey has been concocting soaps, lotions, and perfumes for more than two centuries. Fine craftsmanship and artistic presentation continue as their formula for success.

CÔTÉ BASTIDE

3 rue de Grand Pré

Lourmarin 84160 France

(011) 33 1490 085792

Launched in 1983 with fragrant bars of long-lasting, triple-milled soaps as the company's mainstay, Côté Bastide has expanded to include beautiful bath products of all kinds: creams, salts, talcs, and eaux de toilette. Founder Nicole Houques takes as much pride in the packaging of her French wares as in the products themselves—but these high-quality products are not built on looks alone.

ERBE

196 Prince Street

New York, NY 10012

(212) 966-1445

Stocking European bath and beauty products not likely to be found just anywhere, Erbe has built a loyal following of customers seeking unusual, but useful, cosmetics and such.

FACE

(888) 334-FACE   www.face.com

Easy to apply and easy to wear—with these two directives in mind, mother-daughter team Gun Nowak and Martina Arfwidson set out to develop their own cosmetic company. They succeeded first in Sweden, then brought what they learned with them to the United States.

GIANNA ROSE

18306 Ward Street

Fountain Valley, CA 92708

(888) 544-2662

Wherever you find this creative businesswoman—strolling through the garden, visiting a museum, leafing through a book—Gianna Rose is hard at work, drawing inspiration from the beauty around her for her line of soaps, sachets, and toiletries. Full of wonder for nature, Gianna imbues everything she creates with a touch of garden whimsy.

L'OCCITANE

(888) 623-2880

Available in France since 1976, L'Occitane bath products are now popular the world over thanks to retail stores and a mail-order catalog featuring these attractive wares. The creams, soaps, and shampoos for both women and men are derived from essential oils extracted from organic plants such as lavender and verbena.

NANTUCKET SOAPS

P.O. Box 2115

Nantucket Island, MA 02584

(508) 228-5981

fax: (508) 228-0559

When a former spa owner turns her attentions to developing garden-fresh bath products, the results can be renewing and refreshing. Try Lynn Tucker's soaps, bubble baths, moisturizers, salts, and scrubs and you, too, will feel rejuvenated.

PORTER'S LOTION

(800) 806-1161

Developed over sixty years ago by a local pharmacist in Bozeman, Montana, as a solution for dry skin, the original Porter's lotion is still popular and still effective. Nondrying soaps and oils, together with the lotion, form a complete treatment system.

SEPHORA

(877) SEPHORA

Discover a world of beauty and fragrance at Sephora stores in over twenty locations throughout the United States. These high-style beauty emporiums carry a wide range of products—some made by manufacturers who are world-famous, others who cater to a smaller, boutique trade.

T. LECLERC

(800) 788-4731

Ever since Theophile LeClerc developed his extraordinary French face powders in 1881, they have become legendary for their quality—a perfect shade for every skin type. The company has recently launched a complete collection of cosmetics, including blush, lip color, and eye makeup.

Fragrance

BRANDY PARFUMS, LTD.

1173A Second Avenue

New York, NY 10021-8277

(212) 988-4159

In creating a soothing fragrance with top notes of apple and peach, Patricia Namm had an unusual muse. Her inspiration was Brandy, a friendly palomino quarter horse who steers carriages through New York City's Central Park. The fragrance is a fruit-and-herbal blend with Brandy's likeness on the bottle and box.

CRABTREE AND EVELYN

(800) 624-5211

Made from botanicals and other natural products, the Crabtree and Evelyn line is just what nature intended   bath and beauty products as pure and pretty as possible. Soaps, fragrances, shampoos, and lotions are especially well-regarded by local customers.

DEMETER

27 West Twenty-fourth Street, #200

New York, NY 10010

(800) 482-0422

Devoted to creating subtle scents made from natural materials only, Demeter is known for its line of floral fragrances as well as other single-note scents ranging from fruity to woodsy to grassy. With these familiar fragrances from everyday life, the down-to-earth scents evoke pleasant memories and experiences.

FRAGONARD

20 boulevard Fragonard

Grasse Cedex 06130 France

(011) 33 493 364465

fax: (011) 33 493 365732

Fragonard, a venerable family firm known for delightfully fragrant French wares, produces its scents from Grasse, the heart of Provence's perfume country. Known for its perfumes, bath and body products, and shampoos, Fragonard uses the essence of many flowers to distill the purest fragrance possible.

HOVÉ PARFUMEUR

824 Royal Street

New Orleans, LA 70116

(504) 525-7827

Fragrant with magnolia, lilac, and camelia, Hové bath and beauty products are mixed in the back room of this 1813 town house, using family recipes that are three generations old. Hové perfumes, talcs, and bath oils are softly scented and undeniably luxurious—much like the shop itself.

....

IRENE HIROSE COMPANY

6430 Variel Avenue, #104

Woodland Hills, CA 91367

(818) 222-6647

Dressed in a pretty package and presented with care and attention to detail, Irene Hirose's lovely sachets add scent to closets and drawers. Some of the sachets are even shaped to fit inside a favorite pair of shoes while they're not being worn.

....

JO MALONE

154 Walton Street

London SW3 2JL England

(011) 44 1715 811101

Along Walton Street, a delightful row of shops in London, perfume lovers flock to Jo Malone's door. Customers appreciate Jo's custom-blended fragrances all the more because her exquisite scents are also beautifully packaged.

....

L'ARTISAN PARFUMEUR

(800) 848-6835

The scented creations of L'Artisan Parfumeur—eaux de toilette, room fragrances, and other accessories—include such evocative names as Blackberry Feast, Whispering Leaves, Amber Light,

Under the Fig Tree, Land of Spices, and Out in the Woods. The descriptions and ingredients are closely matched for pure, authentic fragrance.

....

PENHALIGON'S
(011) 44 1818 802050

(800) 588-1992   penhaligons@compuserve.com

Even as a thoroughly modern businesswoman, Sheila Pickles feels a longing for tradition. Her Penhaligon's fragrances combine the best of both worlds with old-fashioned floral scents that appeal to contemporary tastes.

....

THE THYMES LIMITED
(800) 366-4071

Imaginative ideas and artistic packaging are the hallmarks of The Thymes Limited, a fragrance company that relies on flowers, herbs, and other beneficial plants from the garden for its aromatic blends. The line is also known for its soothing, healing properties.

The
PANTRY

Bakers/Bakeries

CONCORD TEACAKES

59 Commonwealth Avenue

West Concord, MA 01742

(978) 369-2409   www.concordteacakes.com

Walk into the Concord Teacakes kitchen and inhale the fragrance of just-baked shortbread and scones. Owner Judy Fersch opened her bakery after she discovered the recipe for one of Emily Dickinson's favorite cakes. On the basis of the success of that recipe alone, Judy expanded her business with other teatime offerings.

DANCING DEER BAKING COMPANY

(888) 699-3337

fax: (617) 442-8118   info@dancingdeer.com

When Dancing Deer opened its doors several years ago, it captured the Boston area by the heart with its all-natural goodies. Now that the bakery has expanded into a mail-order business, others can enjoy these delicious cakes and cookies.

....

DIANE'S BAKERY

23 Bryant Avenue

Roslyn, NY 11576

(516) 621-2522

A sweet partnership began the day chefs Diane Margaritis and John Durkin met. They assumed not only joint cooking careers when they opened a bakery but joint lives as well when they married a short time later. Together, they create tartlets, muffins, tortes, and pies in their old-time, small-town bakery.

....

ECCE PANIS

1126 Third Avenue

New York, NY 10021

(212) 535-2099

"Behold the bread," its name encourages, and customers cheerfully comply. Fresh, crusty loaves—some traditional, some unusual—are turned out daily at this specialty bakery where nothing but the finest flours and ingredients are used.

....

EXTRAORDINARY DESSERTS

2929 Fifth Avenue

San Diego, CA 92103

(619) 294-7001   xdesserts@aol.com

There's not a sweet tooth that can't be satisfied at Extraordinary Desserts, a bakery and café known for outrageous brownies, cakes, and tarts. Owner Karen Krasne relies on tropical fruit flavors for many of her signature treats.

LITTLE PIE COMPANY

424 West Forty-third Street

New York, NY 10036

(877) 872-PIES or (212) 736-4780   www.littlepiecompany.com

Good old-fashioned pies with flaky crusts and irresistibly fresh fillings are turned out daily at Little Pie Company. Owners Arnold Wilkerson and Michael Deraney make sure certain items, such as their mile-high apple pie, are always available while adding seasonal favorites—pumpkin, rhubarb, key lime—to the selection.

MEG RIVERS CAKES

Middle Tysoe

Warwickshire CV35 0SE England

(011) 44 1295 688101

The essence of hearth, home, and the English countryside spells sweet success for baker Meg Rivers. Every bite of a Meg Rivers cake is filled with fruits, nuts, and spices, traditional favorites of the refined English palate. The taste is subtle—not too sweet and not too complex—so true flavors come shining through.

....

PATTICAKES

1900 North Allen Avenue

Altadena, CA 91001

(626) 794-1128

fax: (626) 794-8159

Topped by chocolate scrolls, bows, and flowers, the cakes made by Patricia Murray for her California bakery are a delight to behold. But as every good pastry chef knows, the true test is in the taste, and Patricia's cakes pass with flying colors.

....

PINK ROSE PASTRY SHOP

630 South Fourth Street

Philadelphia, PA 19147

(215) 592-9321

As sweet as the confections it sells, Pink Rose Pastry Shop mixes masterful cakes and pies in a charming setting. Customers are invited to take home these fresh-baked creations or enjoy them on the spot with a cup of hot tea.

....

ROSIE'S CREATIONS

(212) 362-6069

fax: (212) 875-0124

Hand-painted then dotted with icing trim, Ricki Arno's cookies are the perfect dessert, teatime accompaniment, or special-occasion party favor. Ricki takes custom orders for her sugar cookie creations, shaping and coloring them in a variety of ways.

....

SARAH MEADE CAKES

49 Greenwich High Road, Unit 6010

London SE10 8JL England

(011) 44 181 694 2886

fax: (011) 44 181 692 0084

Based on historic recipes, baked in the English countryside, and boxed in special-occasion containers, the cakes of Sarah Meade are known for tradition and taste. No tea table should be set without a lovely tea cake, believes owner Jane Bird, and these fit the bill nicely.

....

THREE TARTS BAKERY

301 South Happ Road

Northfield, IL 60093

(847) 446-5444

Fresh flavors play a starring role at Three Tarts Bakery—in cakes, pies, cookies, truffles, even homemade granola. If it isn't freshly made, it doesn't find its way onto this extensive dessert and bakery menu.

$\mathcal{C}akes$

ANN AMERNICK

(301) 718-0434

Rose blossoms gracefully cascade down the tiers of an Ann Amernick cake, looking as though they were picked at the peak of perfection. This patient pastry chef actually creates these flowery confections in her Maryland kitchen.

COLETTE PETERS

681 Washington Street

New York, NY 10014

(212) 366-6530   cakecolet@aol.com

Cookbook author and cake artist Colette Peters treats cake decorating as an art form. Her master's degree in painting comes in handy as she sculpts and applies delicate trims to her unique cakes, trying to accommodate every bride's special request.

GAIL WATSON CUSTOM CAKES

335 West Thirty-eighth Street

New York, NY 10018

(212) 967-9167   www.gailwatsoncakes.com

A cake by Gail Watson becomes a romantic centerpiece for a special event or occasion. Gail interprets flowers, fabrics, china patterns, monograms, and more in delicious flavors to create her outstanding cake designs.

ISN'T THAT SPECIAL—OUTRAGEOUS CAKES

720 Monroe Street

Hoboken, NJ 07030

(800) 945-6810 or (201) 216-0123   cakediva@aol.com

www.cakediva.com

A former theater student, cake creator Charmaine Jones likes to serve a slice of drama along with her cakes. She embellishes her towering creations with big bouquets of lush, full-blown flowers. Her palette ranges from softly pastel to boldly bright.

JAN KISH LA PETIT FLEUR

P.O. Box 872

Worthington, OH 43085

(614) 848-5855

Jan Kish bakes special-occasion cakes that are always showstoppers, drawing inspiration from nature's garden. Wildflowers, leaves, and butterflies often provide inspiration, but Jan can create almost any motif in painstaking detail.

RON BEN-ISRAEL CAKES

130 West Twenty-fifth Street, 2nd Floor

New York, NY 10001

(212) 627-2418 (by appointment only)

cakemaster@weddingcakes.com

www.weddingcakes.com

Garlanded in bands of flowers, ribbon, and other exquisite details, Ron Ben-Israel's cakes are often the hit of a party. Everything that graces one of Ron's cakes is edible, but guests often choose to save the amazing sugar flowers as keepsakes.

SYLVIA WEINSTOCK CAKES, LTD.

273 Church Street

New York, NY 10013

(212) 925-6698

The exquisite sugar flowers created by this talented cake artist are so real, it's not surprising Sylvia studies botanical guidebooks to create her cake embellishments. Customers' requests for roses, lilies of the valley, tulips, and freesia are happily accommodated.

Caterers

BONNE BOUCHE

P.O. Box 1573

Capitola, CA 95010

(831) 479-9637   bbouche@aol.com

While many caterers bring plain white linens and standard-issue tableware to their events, Bonne Bouche makes sure the accessories are as special as the cuisine. Owners Aimee Murphy and Karen Aulback set an exquisite table on which to present their memorable meals.

DESIGN CUISINE

2659 South Shirlington Road

Arlington, VA 22206

(703) 979-9400   www.designcuisine.com

Design Cuisine's chefs specialize in meals artfully prepared and presented from their commercial kitchen. The cooking crew knows just the right seasonings to use to make flavors come alive.

LOAVES AND FISHES

P.O. Box 318

Sagaponack, NY 11962

(516) 537-0555

This gourmet food shop owned by a mother-daughter duo caters savory meals for special occasions. Anna and Sybille Pump team up to turn fresh fruits, herbs, and vegetables into delicious dishes, some of which they offer at their Main Street shop.

NEW ENGLAND CATERING COMPANY

415 Sharon-Goshen Turnpike

West Cornwall, CT 06796

(203) 672-6554

Patrons in quest of a gracious meal find just what they're looking for when New England Catering Company does the food preparation. Regional recipes using fresh local ingredients are the specialty here.

Chocolates/Candies

BE-SPECKLED TROUT

422 Hudson Street

New York, NY 10014

(212) 255-1421

A visit to Be-Speckled Trout is like stepping into the corner candy store from days long gone by. With old-fashioned fixtures and furnishings from the past, the shop resembles every child's dream of the friendliest place in the world to spend his or her savings on a sack of penny candy.

BEST FRIENDS COCOA

P.O. Box 157

Newton Highlands, MA 02161

(781) 329-8800

Turning a mutual love of chocolate into a thriving business, Karen Levine and Naomi Storm feel they have found their calling. These longtime friends have developed just the right formula for what they call the ultimate cup of cocoa, packaging their mix in delightful boxes and tins.

BURDICK CHOCOLATES

P.O. Box 593, Main Street

Walpole, NH 03608

(800) 229-2419

fax: (603) 756-4326

High-quality chocolates and the freshest possible ingredients are in the excellent hands of a master chocolatier at Burdick. Truffles and other extraordinary dishes are crafted and created in the grand traditions of the best European confectioners.

DOROTHY TIMBERLAKE CANDIES

Main Street

Eaton Center, NH 03849

(603) 447-2221

Using a teakettle, spoon, and antique molds as her only tools, Dorothy Timberlake creates colorful hard candies and lollipops from her pristine candy kitchen in the Northeast. The candies are delicious to nibble but are also appropriate as festive ornaments or as package trims.

ELIZABETH HARRISON CHOCOLATES

Available through Eureka (719) 475-0135

http://members.aol.com/eurekagift

Decorated with delicately piped rosebuds, beads, starbursts, garlands, and lattice, these special-occasion chocolates gleam like the jewels in a Fabergé egg. Such exquisite confections are especially well suited to Easter, Christmas, and Valentine's Day.

FIDDLE FERN CHOCOLATIER

278 Green River Road

Alford, MA 01230

(413) 528-2563

Both tasty and tasteful, Fiddle Fern's handmade, hand-cut fudge (available with or without roasted walnuts) resembles fine imported truffles of the highest quality. Made with fresh ingredients and fine chocolate, the fudge is packaged in an attractive keepsake tin; pieces are also available boxed as party and wedding favors.

NEUHAUS

27 Gallerie de la Reine

1000 Brussels, Belgium

(011) 322 512 6359

Candy connoisseurs have long appreciated the rich flavor of Belgian chocolates, and those made by Neuhaus are among the most sought after in the world. One of Europe's oldest confectioners now sells its heavenly wares at boutiques in the United States.

NORTHERN CHOCOLATES

2034 North Martin Luther King Drive (at Third Street)

Milwaukee, WI 53212

(414) 372-1885

Available from the store only (no mail-order business), Northern Chocolates are shaped in antique molds by Milwaukee chocolatier Jim Fetzer. Many of his molds are over one hundred years old, making his unusual shapes as special as the chocolates themselves.

....

ROGERS CHOCOLATES

913 Government Street

Victoria, BC V8W 1X5 Canada

(250) 384-7021   sales@rogerschocolates.com

www.rogerschocolates.com

Called Victoria creams after the town in which they're made, the soft-center chocolate candies that have made Rogers Chocolates famous are available in many flavors. Orange, maple, raspberry, and mint are just a few of the long-standing favorites, available at the store and through mail order.

Gourmet Foods

BELLA VISTA FARM

2850 Sixty-third Street

Fennville, MI 49408

(616) 857-7400

Inspired by stories of other fruit farmers around the country, John and Nancy Renaldi left their jobs in Chicago and bought a farm of their own in Fennville, Michigan. Here they harvest organically grown apples and berries from a ten-acre spread, turning out jars of delicious jams.

....

BLACK HOUND

170 Second Avenue

New York, NY 10009

(800) 344-4417

Whether you visit the Black Hound store or shop from their catalog, you'll be tempted by their distinct delectables: honey-toasted almonds, cheese sticks, chocolate truffles, brownies, butter cookies, and more—all freshly made and handsomely packaged.

CHARLOTTE'S STEAMED PUDDINGS

P.O. Box 250, Hill Road

Alstead, NH 03602

(603) 835-6519   anderwill@cheshire.net   www.heritagefood.com

A deep, dark, rich taste is the hallmark of these plum and steamed puddings, made in midsummer to ensure plenty of time for aging to perfection. Using an old family recipe, Leslie Honey has expanded her repertoire somewhat, adding innovative flavors such as ginger, currant, and maple.

EMILY RIDLEY'S JAM

P.O. Box 487

Cambridge CB3 8FW England

(011) 44 1954 789123

fax: (011) 44 1954 789779

An old family business in rural Essex is as revered as ever for its famous jams, jellies, and preserves. The line includes over two dozen flavors that make tasty spreads for biscuits, popovers, muffins, and scones or welcome additions to dessert recipes.

KATZ AND COMPANY
(800) 676-7176

From California's Napa Valley, Kim and Albert Katz concoct delicious honeys, olive oils, and preserves using the freshest fruits grown on local farms. All of the fruits are free of pesticides, adding to the just-harvested taste.

MOTHERS AND OTHERS
P.O. Box 837

Guilford, ME 04443

(207) 876-4737

Homemade pansy cookies and other flowery fare are baked daily by Mothers and Others, a small business in Maine giving jobs to mothers living in rural areas and thereby boosting the community and local economy.

PAXTON AND WHITFIELD, LTD.
93 Jermyn Street

London SW1Y 6JE England

(011) 44 1719 300259   www.cheesemongers.co.uk

This venerable purveyor of cheeses from around the world is especially well known for a wide range of English cheeses, including

Stilton, Wensleydale, Derby, and Cheshire. Proud holders of the Queen's royal warrant, Paxton and Whitfield has been in business since 1797.

....

ROBERT ROTHSCHILD BERRY FARM
P.O. Box 311
Urbana, OH 43078
(800) 356-8933   www.robertrothschild.com
    This family-owned business consistently produces award-winning gourmet food products using farm-fresh raspberries. Vinegar, salsa, chutney, and other condiments are flavored with raspberries picked at the peak of flavor.

Teas/Tearooms

ABC PARLOUR CAFE
38 East Nineteenth Street
New York, NY 10003
(212) 677-2233   www.abchome.com
    In a grand old emporium in lower Manhattan lies a hidden treasure beckoning shoppers to stop and enjoy a spot of tea. After browsing the many floors of antiques and furnishings at ABC Carpet and Home, visitors find the Parlour Cafe to be just the place for a brief respite.

....

ACCOUTREMENTS BY LIZA

P.O. Box 6008

Fullerton, CA 92834

(800) 554-6624   www.cataloguecity.com

A mail-order catalog devoted to the pleasant art of taking tea, these pages are filled with cups and saucers, strainers, teapots, and trays—all kinds of accessories related to teatime.

CHARLESTON TEA PLANTATION

6617 Maybank Highway

Wadmalaw Island, SC 29487

(800) 443-5987   chastea@awod.com

On a lush plantation near Charleston, South Carolina, fresh tea leaves are harvested, dried, cut, and blended by an enterprising team of horticulturalists. Charleston Tea is a rare hybrid—not only is the famous orange-pekoe variety delicious, but all of it is grown on American shores.

EASTERN SHORE TEA COMPANY

(800) 542-6064

Jan and Howard Burns, founders of Maryland's Eastern Shore Tea Company, make over forty delicate tea blends, one for just about every tea-drinking mood. Flavored with vanilla, jasmine, lavender, mint, and rose petals, these unique teas offer subtle nuance with every sip.

HARNEY AND SONS FINE TEAS
Salisbury, CT
(800) TEA TIME

John Harney and his sons Michael and Paul are the master blenders here, where a shared love of tea has become a family tradition—and passion. From the charming New England town of Salisbury, the Harneys share their knowledge of fine blends with tours and tastings.

HEART OF AMERICA/GRACIOUS LIVING
370 West Bridge Street
New Hope, PA 18938
(215) 862-3304

An inviting place in a friendly, picturesque town, Heart of America offers a delightful option for those who enjoy both shopping and taking tea. With home accessories filling the shelves and a modicum of tea paraphernalia added in, Melinda Kuehne creates a masterful mix of both.

LADY PRIMROSE'S
The Crescent
500 Crescent Court
Dallas, TX 75201
(800) 525-5066 or (214) 871-8333

Assembling and condensing the best of Britain was the goal of owners Caroline Rose Hunt and Vivian Young when they opened their Dallas shop and tearoom Lady Primrose's. They have met that goal with much success and continue to exceed the expectations of even the most devoted Anglophiles.

....

MACKENZIE–CHILDS BUTLER'S PANTRY

824 Madison Avenue

New York, NY 10021

(212) 570-6050

Known for whimsical shapes, colors, and flourishes, the pottery at MacKenzie-Childs steals the show at their flagship store in New York City. But look a little further and you'll discover more hidden gems just waiting to be found. Take a trip to the second floor and you'll find afternoon tea about to be served.

....

MCCHARLES HOUSE TEAROOM

335 South C Street

Tustin, CA 92780

(714) 731-4063

tea@mccharleshouse.com   www.mccharleshouse.com

For a quiet afternoon interlude, head to this cozy cottage, where hosts Audrey and Vivian Heredia are known for providing tea with all the trimmings. "We put British afternoon tea on an American schedule to accommodate everyone's hours," says Audrey of the convenient policy of serving tea all through the day.

....

ROSE TREE COTTAGE

828 East California Boulevard

Pasadena, CA 91107

(626) 793-3337   www.rosetreecottage.com

With formal training in the preparation and presentation of a proper English tea, shop owners Mary and Edmund Fry indulge their customers in a bit of British etiquette along with tasty teas and treats. After taking tea, visitors can shop among shelves upon shelves of gifts and goodies.

WINDSOR COURT HOTEL

300 Gravier Street

New Orleans, LA 70130

(800) 262-2662   www.windsorcourthotel.com

The quiet charm of the tearoom at the esteemed Windsor Court Hotel in New Orleans is just what shoppers and neighbors seek when they tuck in for afternoon tea. The setting is serene and the menu is four-star, making this a top choice with tea drinkers in the know.

WORD OF MOUTH

1012 Lexington Avenue

New York, NY 10021

(212) 734-9483   www.citysearch.com/nyc/cafewordofmouth

Expect all the fixings at Word of Mouth's teatime café, a second-story refuge serving favorites from chef Christi Finch's superb take-out menu. The best dishes available downstairs are served daily in this calm, quiet restaurant on New York City's Upper East Side.

Wines/Vineyards

CHAPPELLET

1581 Sage Canyon Road

St. Helena, CA 94574

(707) 963-7136   info@chappellet.com   www.chappellet.com

Planted on a rocky Napa Valley hillside, Pritchard Hill is a dream come true for Molly and Donn Chappellet, who harvest sauvignon and other varieties of grapes for some of California's best wines.

IRON HORSE

9786 Ross Station Road

Sebastopol, CA 95472

(707) 887-1507   www.ironhorsevineyards.com

Fine wines are the family legacy at California's Iron Horse Vineyards, where Audrey and Barry Sterling share their love of wine making with their two grown children, who have a hand in turning out carefully tended wines.

NANCY'S WINES FOR FOOD

313 Columbus Avenue

New York, NY 10023

(212) 877-4040

Known for her tasteful choices for partnering food and wine, Nancy Maniscalco has built a unique niche for herself in the wine business. Her shop is as tasteful as her wine selections, a neighborhood establishment that reaches far beyond its Upper West Side location.

....

PERRIER-JOUËT

Epernay, France

(011) 33 326 533800

In Epernay, France's champagne capital, Perrier-Jouët is blended, fermented, bottled, and aged, upholding long-standing traditions associated with the world's most famous wine. Claiming that champagne turns every meal into a festive occasion, the vintners share Perrier-Jouët's history with visitors who call in advance to schedule a tour.

....

SCHRAMSBERG

1400 Schramsberg Road

Calistoga, CA 94515

(707) 942-4558   schramsberg@aol.com   www.schramsberg.com

There's always cause for celebration at Schramsberg Vineyard, where sparkling wines are produced from grapes that have grown here since 1880. The soil and conditions are just right for these varietals, which are pressed and then fermented twice in the traditional champenoise tradition.

....

SUTTER HOME

P.O. Box 248

St. Helena, CA 94574

(707) 963-3104   info@sutterhome.com   www.sutterhome.com

The renowned red and white zinfandels of Sutter Home have earned this Napa Valley vineyard international acclaim. The delicate blush wine is a startling contrast to the spicy red with its deep hues and rich aroma.

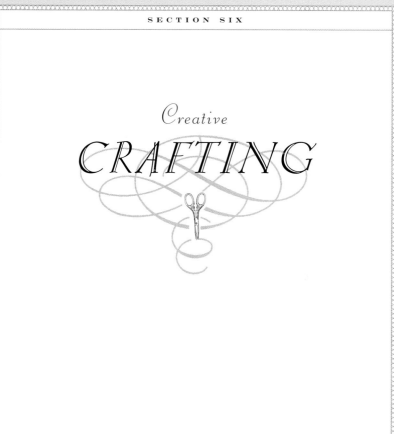

Creative
CRAFTING

Art/Artists

CROCKER HILL STUDIO

45 King Street

St. Andrews

New Brunswick E0G 2X0 Canada

(888) 255-4251   crohill@nbnet.nb.ca

Nature reigns at Crocker Hill Studio, the garden workshop of Steven and Gail Smith. Birds and flowers come to life in renderings by these two nature-loving artists.

DEBORAH CHABRIAN

(800) 927-2505

Capturing moments both imagined and real, Deborah Chabrian's style lends itself to spontaneous interpretation. She often embellishes a watercolor painting with her own additions, making sure the color and light are just right to enhance what she observes.

DEBORAH SCHENCK

Kipling Hill Road, Box 221D

Stratford, VT 05072

(802) 387-4204

Artist Deborah Schenck takes care to craft works on paper that communicate her painterly vision of nature. Her work looks hand painted, but her technique involves applying a Polaroid transfer image to textured paper.

DENNIS KYTE

P.O. Box 215

Washington Depot, CT 06794

fax: (860) 868-9336

Watercolorist Dennis Kyte revives the venerable art of botanical illustration, adding his own whimsical update: His botanicals take the form of flowery shoes. From sunflowers and daffodils to daylilies and forget-me-nots, Dennis's "footwear" is truly petal soft.

LESLEY HOLMES

Harvey House

High Street

Moreton in Marsh

Gloucester GL56 0AT England

(011) 44 1608 650662 (by appointment only)

Artist Lesley Holmes finds her muse in the Cotswolds, an area in England filled with romantic cottages and fanciful village life. The region is fresh and alive, and Lesley captures its unique and unmistakable charm in watercolor.

MARTY WHALEY ADAMS GALLERY

120 Meeting Street

Charleston, SC 29401

(843) 853-8512   martywadams@mindspring.com

www.martywadams.com

As one of *Victoria*'s artists in residence, Marty Whaley Adams created prints and posters capturing the essence of Southern charm. From her Charleston studio, Marty continues the tradition of painting lovely still lifes that convey the best of Southern style.

MARY AZARIAN

258 Gray Road

Plainfield, VT 05667

(802) 454-8087   mazarian@together.net

Vermont artist Mary Azarian carves country memories in the woodcuts she makes of rural scenes and nearby gardens. Her love of nature and old-fashioned flowers is immediately apparent when her work is viewed on posters, note cards, and catalog covers.

....

MARYJO KOCH

555 Martin Road

Santa Cruz, CA 95060

(408) 425-7422

Always amazed by the enchantments of nature, artist Maryjo Koch spends her days sketching and painting the endless wonders of Northern California. Maryjo also teaches a variety of art classes on topics ranging from water botanicals to leaves and vegetables.

....

SARAH LUGG

(011) 44 1714 333321   loveart@globalnet.co.uk

English artist Sarah Lugg creates images straight from the heart—sentimental expressions that capture her lighthearted way with words in the found materials she loves to collect.

....

TRISHA ROMANCE

P.O. Box 1321, 177 King Street

Niagara-on-the-Lake, Ontario L0S 1J0 Canada

(800) 667-8525

With a deeply felt love of family and a strong sense of tradition, Trisha Romance paints scenes familiar to all of us—children gathered around the dining table, a mother reading a bedtime story, the warm glow of a home filled with love. Trisha knows her subject matter intimately, often using her own children as inspiration.

Buttons

GRANDMOTHER'S BUTTONS

9814 Royal Street

St. Francisville, LA 70775

(504) 635-4107   gbuttons@bsf.net

By rescuing antique buttons from obscurity, Susan Davis has launched both a successful business and a button museum. Grandmother's Buttons, located in an old bank in this small Southern town, sells and displays outstanding examples of button art.

LULU'S

405 North Main Street

Royal Oak, MI 48067

(248) 542-6464

Known for her button embellishments, Lulu Cameron crafts unique gifts and greeting cards combining buttons with vintage photographs. The images she chooses have the same old-fashioned patina as the buttons themselves.

MY MOTHER'S BUTTONS

21221 Shell Valley Road

Edmonds, WA 98026

(425) 778-3693

A windfall of antique buttons from her mother gave Linda Meagher an idea for a business that has been blossoming ever since.

My Mother's Buttons takes finds from the sewing box and turns them into brooches, bracelets, and barrettes.

RENAISSANCE BUTTONS

826 West Armitage Avenue

Chicago, IL 60614

(773) 883-9508   www.renaissancebuttons.com

Gathering buttons from around the world, Sarah McGovern opened Renaissance Buttons in a Victorian building on a tree-lined street in Chicago. Inside the shop are the jet, brass, pearl, and china buttons that once adorned clothing—and lives—of the past.

TENDER BUTTONS

143 East Sixty-second Street

New York, NY 10021

(212) 758-7004

Button seekers and collectors the world over flock to this address to search through an extensive collection of old and new designs. Tender Buttons, located in a restored brownstone, houses enamel, porcelain, ceramic, and glass buttons—some museum quality, all creatively displayed.

Crafts/Sewing

ANNE POWELL, LTD.

(561) 287-3007   info@annepowellltd.com   www.annepowellltd.com

Looking for a brass thimble in a special size? A rug-hooking needle with a wooden handle? How about a darning egg or a quilting frame with a hoop? Anne Powell, Ltd., can provide sewers with all their stitching needs—everything from embroidery scissors to pincushions.

CLAIRE MURRAY

(800) 252-4733   www.clairemurray.com

Inspired by the herbs and flowers she loves, Claire Murray brings her gardens to life on colorful hooked pillows and rugs that are her trademark. What started as an innocent hobby has become a flourishing enterprise with shops scattered across the country.

DMC

10 Port Kearny

South Kearny, NJ 07032

(973) 589-0606

To needleworkers around the world, the name DMC is synonymous with fine thread. And after 250 years in business, DMC is especially proud of the traditions associated with its yarns and threads, allowing crocheting, embroidery, knitting, and quilting projects to be their absolute best.

EHRMAN TAPESTRY

(888) 826-8600   usehrman@clark.net   www.ehrmantapestry.com

Known for elegant needlepoint kits, this English company combines high-quality materials with excellent design in everything it creates. Stitchers have come to recognize—and appreciate—the artful colors and compositions Ehrman consistently produces.

....

ELIZABETH BRADLEY DESIGN, LTD.

1 West End

Beaumaris

Anglesey LL58 8BD North Wales

(800) 635-0974 or (011) 44 1248 811 055   ebd@elizabethbradley.co.uk

Well-loved by beginners and experts alike, these needlepoint designs are often adapted from vintage textiles and antique china. The kits feature the finest in yarns and materials.

....

ERICA WILSON

717 Madison Avenue

New York, NY 10021

(212) 832-7290

Many stitchers consider Erica Wilson's tasteful, elegant designs the ultimate in handmade chic. The acknowledged queen of needlepoint in many stitching circles, Erica accommodates custom work as easily as the kits she sells in her shop.

....

MARGARET MURTON

Castlemount

53 Leicester Road

Ashby de la Zouch

Leicestershire LE6 5DD England

(011) 44 1530 414460

Amid piles of wool heaped in baskets in her studio, Margaret Murton sketches fruit-and-floral motifs that are translated into needlework tapestries and embroideries. Margaret takes great delight in the minutiae of nature, celebrating her observations in canvas and yarn.

Custom Services

FRANK VAN VALKENBURG PORTRAITS

491 West Main Street

Danville, VA 24541

(804) 799-4635

This Danville, Virginia, photographer captures the joy of childhood in simple settings and poses that make his subjects especially memorable. Specializing in portraits of children, Frank brings years of experience to each sitting.

HARRY EBERHARDT AND SON, INC.

2010 Walnut Street

Philadelphia, PA 19103

(215) 568-4144

The family members who now operate this century-old firm

claim to be America's oldest and largest dealers in, and artistic restorers of, porcelain and glassware. Since 1888 this reputable Philadelphia firm has mended countless pieces of broken china, restoring irreplaceable artifacts and family treasures with the care they deserve.

....

LACIS

2982 Adeline Street

Berkeley, CA 94703

(510) 843-7178   www.lacis.com

A deep concern for lace—its care and preservation—drives Kaethe Kliot to take on the restoration of wedding dresses, tablecloths, christening gowns, and other meaningful family textiles. "Restoration ensures that laces will have a new life so they may be used, and enjoyed, again and again." This is the mission at Lacis, Kaethe's Berkeley, California, storefront.

....

MARY ANDERSON DECOUPAGE

270 Riverside Drive

New York, NY 10025

(212) 865-8370

An inveterate clipper, Mary Anderson found a way to turn her passion to profit when she started designing decoupage plates using decorative paper designs. Mary loves using a client's personal photos in her work, especially when commemorating a special birthday or anniversary.

....

STELLA ALBERTI

465 South Sherbourne Drive

Los Angeles, CA 90048

(310) 550-8530

Using nothing more than needle and thread, Stella turns plain fabric into elegant handmades embellished with French knots, satin stitches, and more. All embroidery is worked entirely by hand.

Handmades

GRANNY MADE

381 Amsterdam Avenue

New York, NY 10024

(212) 496-1222

At Granny Made, shoppers find an outstanding array of sweaters and hand knits for women and children. Styles come and go with each season, remaining ever fashionable and well made.

OUT OF THE PAST

9012 Third Avenue

Brooklyn, NY 11209

(718) 748-1490

Exacting workmanship, careful stitches—these are the hallmarks of vintage handmades. In Brooklyn, New York, a shop preserves these needlework traditions by applying old-fashioned standards to today's handmades. Out of the Past creates a unique reputation for itself by reworking antique clothing and textiles for use today.

TIMELESS TREASURES

Main Street, P.O. Box 4277

Vineyard Haven, MA 02568

(508) 696-7637

Irish knits keep customers returning to this well-stocked store, where the wares are handmade and imported from Ireland. Owner Gerda O'Rourke tells customers they can never have too many sweaters in their wardrobes—and with styles like these, she's right.

Ribbon

BLOOMERS

2975 Washington Street

San Francisco, CA 94115

(415) 563-3266

A shop devoted almost exclusively to ribbons, Bloomers offers a dazzling array that takes one's breath away. The display includes a large inventory of antique designs as well as brand-new iridescent, imported, and wire-trimmed ribbons.

CREAM CITY RIBBON

181 North Broadway

Milwaukee, WI 53202

(414) 277-1221   ccr@creamcityribbon.com   www.creamcityribbon.com

Crisp, papery, and flat, the biodegradable cotton ribbons designed and developed by Lorette Russenberger are not only environmentally friendly but charmingly old-fashioned, too.

HYMAN HENDLER

67 West Thirty-eighth Street

New York, NY 10018

(212) 840-8393

The grandfather of all ribbon stores, this one boasts one of the largest selections of old-fashioned and newfangled designs. Ribbons have never gone out of style here, where the ribbon trade remains alive and well.

RIBBONRY

119 Louisiana Avenue

Perrysburg, OH 43551

(419) 872-0073   info@ribbonry.com   www.ribbonry.com

When wrapped in her signature ribbons, a gift from Camela Nitschke is twice as nice: The package itself is usually as special as the gift within. Camela sells yardages of ribbons and trims in almost any length from her quaint shop in Perrysburg, Ohio.

RIBBONS BY DIANA KRIEG

1 Old Middlefield Road

Mountain View, CA 94043

(888) 893-6782 or (650) 940-1152

Armed with an incurable love of color and textiles, Diana Krieg used to collect ribbons; now she sells them—as adornments on handmade sachets and other pretty accessories.

Yarns

CASTLEGATE FARM

424 Kingwood-Locktown Road

Flemington, NJ 08822

(908) 996-6152   castlegatefarm@juno.com

Castlegate Farm is legendary for the soft, lustrous fleece that is spun into virgin wool yarn for beautiful caps and sweaters. Owner Nancy Oliver Clarke not only spins the yarns, she also designs the cable, crew, and polo patterns.

LA KNITTERIE PARISIENNE

(818) 766-1515

Designer and shop owner Edith Eig makes it her job to teach everyone, including children, the joys of knitting. Using the stylish yarns she stocks, Edith encourages her customers to create beautiful garments that are priceless because they are handmade.

LISA PARKS KNITS

7 North Saginaw Street

Pontiac, MI 48342

(248) 332-1313

fax: (248) 332-1531

In Lisa's shop, fashionable yarns and stylish sweaters compete for attention as customers wander the aisles. "I was always good at knitting and wanted to make things people could really enjoy wearing," says Lisa, who has met the challenge by introducing this enjoyable craft into the lives of today's busy women.

....

RIO GRANDE WEAVERS SUPPLY

216B Pueblo Norte

Taos, NM 87571

(800) 765-1272   weaving@taos.newmex.com

www.taosweb.com/weaving

Hand-dyed natural yarns turn even the easiest handmade projects into sophisticated wearables. Artist Rachel Brown's yarns are dipped in color up to four times so subtle gradations result.

....

TRICOTER

3121 East Madison Street

Seattle, WA 98112

(206) 328-6505   tricoter@aol.com   www.tricoter.com

Colorful, fashionable yarns that click with knitters are the specialty of the house at Tricoter in Seattle. Stylish patterns and expert instruction are also available so customers can truly tend to their own knitting.

HOLIDAYS and
GIFT GIVING

Bookstores

ARCHIVIA

944 Madison Avenue

New York, NY 10021

(212) 439-9194   www.archivia.com

In this stylish city bookstore, a very specific point of view is expressed through the design, garden, and architecture titles on display. Owners Joan Gers and Cynthia Conigliaro specialize in books on the decorative arts in an atmosphere conducive to the subjects they love.

BIOGRAPHY BOOK SHOP

400 Bleecker Street

New York, NY 10014

(212) 807-8655

As its name implies, this cozy shop specializes in biographies of all kinds. Customers also find many other titles of interest, satisfying readers of all persuasions.

....

COOKBOOK COTTAGE

1279 Bardstown Road

Louisville, KY 40204

(502) 458-5227

When looking for the oldest, latest, or rarest in cookbooks, wise shoppers know to look here first. Cookbook Cottage is as cozy as its name—a "library" specializing in culinary classics. Customers are encouraged to browse as well as buy.

....

HARD TO FIND NEEDLEWORK BOOKS

96 Roundwood Road

Newton, MA 02464

(617) 969-0942   hardtofind@needleworkbooks.com

www.needleworkbooks.com

The name of this business aptly describes its specialty. Stitchers the world over use this valuable resource to track down the titles they need, no matter how obscure or rare.

....

KITCHEN ARTS AND LETTERS

1435 Lexington Avenue

New York, NY 10128

(212) 876-5550

This specialty bookstore boasts the most extensive collection of cooking-related titles under one roof. Chefs and hobbyists are likely to find exactly what they're searching for at Kitchen Arts and Letters, whether brand new or out-of-print, especially with such able assistance from the sales staff.

THE MILL

P.O. Box 232, Fairmount Road East

Pottersville, NJ 07979

(908) 439-2724   cummins@panix.com

In a restored landmark mill, antique book dealers James and Carol Cummins have set up shop, dealing with treasured volumes that are found all over the world and sold to customers across the country.

THREE LIVES AND COMPANY

154 West Tenth Street

New York, NY 10014

(212) 741-2069

A trip to Three Lives and Company and a chance to wander among the bookshelves is a welcome pleasure. The worthy diversions here include poetry, biographies, story collections, anthologies, and volumes handpicked by owners Jill Dunbar and Jenny Feder to provide customers with the constant companionship of books.

....

URSUS BOOKS

981 Madison Avenue

New York, NY 10021

(212) 772-8787

ursus@ursusbooks.com   www.ursusbooks.com

Peter and Evelyn Kraus delight in turning over old leaves—some rare, some simply beautiful—and introducing collectors to the fine world of books and decorative prints. Their New York City store specializes in just such wonderful wares.

Children and Babies

....

AMIANA

(212) 254-3914   amianaltd@worldnet.att.net

www.amianafootwear.com

For special dress-up occasions, girls from six to twelve years old love Amiana's high-fashion party clothes and shoes.

....

AUNTIE BARBARA ANTIQUES

238 South Beverly Drive

Beverly Hills, CA 90212

(310) 285-0873

After years of collecting the things she loved—antique clothing and accessories, quilts, layettes—Barbara Bartman decided to start her own store, opening the door to a charming new career and business along the way.

....

BRIGID CHILDREN'S CLOTHES

49 Audrey Avenue

Oyster Bay, NY 11771

(516) 922-6009

   This three-year-old shop features classic clothing for kids designed exclusively for and available only at Brigid. Sizes range from infant to size twelve. Those who know and love the line say the styles are simple, the fabrics outstanding—a perfect combination when outfitting little ones.

....

BUCKINGHAM MERCHANTILE

466 South Coast Highway 101

Encinitas, CA 92024

(760) 436-7666

   The clothes at Buckingham Merchantile, a delightful children's shop in Encinitas, California, are not only sturdy, classic, and cute, they're also sensibly sized by weight. Owner Gail Smith-Peterson takes the guesswork out of sizing for mothers and others shopping for irresistible baby gifts.

....

CANTERBURY BEARS, LTD.

The Old Coach House

Courthill, Littleborn

Canterbury, Kent CT3 1XU England

(011) 44 1227 728238

Little did artist John Blackburn know when he designed his first teddy bear almost twenty years ago that "Flash" would preside over an entire company of bears. John's family of Canterbury bears is now collected all over the world—by adults and children alike.

ISABEL GARRETON, INC.

4061 Miraleste Drive

Palos Verdes, CA 90275

(310) 833-7768

fax: (310) 833-8224

When Isabel Garreton started her clothing company twelve years ago, it was her hope to provide pretty fashions for young girls. With styles that combine tradition with a dash of hand embroidery—and always a measure of youthful whimsy—she has more than succeeded.

LITTLE FOLK ART, INC.

1120 Montana Avenue

Santa Monica, CA 90403

(310) 576-0909

fax: (310) 576-0440

After determining what the rooms of children's dreams would look like, Susan Salzman set out to create the real-life furnishings. Her beds, chests, wardrobes, and stools are winsome and winning—and make a transition nicely to other uses when youngsters are grown.

....

MONICA NOEL

23 Benedict Place

Greenwich, CT 06830

(203) 661-0505

fax: (203) 661-1035   monicanoel@aol.com

Fine fabrics and exquisite hand-smocking turn these children's clothes, sized from infants through age ten, into wearable works of art. Christening gowns, robes, and party dresses are the specialties.

....

PLAIN JANE

525 Amsterdam Avenue

New York, NY 10024

(212) 595-6916

With a fresh take on tradition, everything old is new again at this Manhattan children's boutique: fanciful quilts, stylish clothes, comfy furniture, and clever toys. Relying on inspiration from the handmades they collect and covet, shop owners Suzanne O'Brien and Melanie Williams sell only that which is well made and long lasting.

....

SOPHIE FOX SHOP

404 North Robertson Boulevard

Los Angeles, CA 90048

(310) 659-6929

Little girls find their heart's desire at this magical Los Angeles store. Tutus, mary janes, hair bows, and flower girl dresses fill this enchanting emporium, inviting children to enter the wonderful world of dress-up.

THROUGH THE LOOKING GLASS

3802 Roswell Road

Atlanta, GA 30342

(404) 231-4007

Marketing savvy and motherhood are a magical mix for Trina Summins, owner of this favorite Atlanta shop for children's clothes. Trina left a job in retail when her children were born, but now uses the skills she learned to steer her own boutique full speed ahead.

WICKER GARDEN BABY

1327 Madison Avenue

New York, NY 10128

(212) 410-7001

Owner Pamela Scurry indulges her love of luxury with enchanting clothing and furniture designs for infants and young-sters. Well-crafted cribs, changing tables, and rockers mix with layettes, buntings, and sweaters in this wonderful world of children.

Christmas and Special Occasions

CHRISTOPHER RADKO

(800) 71 RADKO

Distinguished by their intricate detail, brilliant color, and ample size, ornaments by Christopher Radko are adapted from antique molds and handblown by Eastern European glassblowers. These glittering reproductions are so authentic, it's hard to tell them apart from the old ones.

MARGARET FURLONG DESIGNS

210 State Street

Salem, OR 97301

(800) 255-3114

One look at designer Margaret Furlong's porcelain shells, angels, stars, hearts, and suns, and there's no doubt what inspires this nature-loving artist. She takes her favorite symbols from nature and crafts them into simply elegant ornaments of the season.

NANCY ROSIN

P.O. Box 647

Franklin Lakes, NJ 07417

(201) 337-5834

fax: (201) 337-3356   nancyrosin@aol.com

www.telebody.com/valentines

Over the years, collector Nancy Rosin has amassed such a unique collection of paper cards, valentines, and other ephemera from the past that her collection stands out among dealers and collectors in the know as one of the finest.

....

OLD WORLD CHRISTMAS

(800) 962-7669

Whether hung individually or en masse, Old World Christmas ornaments are completely mesmerizing—a magnificent re-creation of opalescent, hand-painted glass ornaments of the nineteenth century. Beth and Tim Merck have proudly returned to the tradition of producing German-style ornaments of exquisite workmanship.

AROMA NATURALS

1202 McGaw Avenue

Irvine, CA 92614

(800) 462-7662

fax: (800) 955-9481   www.aromanaturals.com

With the goal of creating the purest, most natural aroma candles available, Aroma Naturals handcrafts candles of the utmost freshness and quality. These are made from 100 percent essential oils (no synthetic fragrance is used) to deliver the most therapeutic benefits possible.

....

BELL'OCCHIO

8 Brady Street

San Francisco, CA 94103

(415) 864-4048   www.bellocchio.com

Translated as "an eye for the beautiful," Bell'occhio is indeed a place of beauty. Owners Claudia Schwartz and Toby Hanson seek a wide assortment of whimsies and wonders for their store—cards, books, jewelry, gift wrap—all of it chosen for its intrinsic beauty.

BRAVURA

(415) 474-9092

fax: (415) 474-9093

From her San Francisco studio, Denise Fiedler turns out unique accessories for women—travel bags, cosmetic cases, sachets, shoe bags—to help them stay well organized in the prettiest possible way. Her designs are often silk-screened, sometimes trimmed with ribbon flowers, and usually carry a touch of handwork to finish each stunning creation.

BUNNIES BY THE BAY

3115 V Place

Anacortes, WA 98221

(360) 293-8037   bunny@bunniesbythebay.com

www.bunniesbythebay.com

Known for cuddly critters, Bunnies by the Bay is a winsome world where lively imaginations take hold. Fans of these whimsical

designs always find a creative assortment of plush handmade rabbits and accessories, designed by sisters Krystal Kirkpatrick and Suzanne Knutson.

C'EST LA VIE

24 Atlantic Avenue

Marblehead, MA 01945

(781) 639-2468   clvmhead@aol.com

C'est la Vie, a shop full of whimsy, features charming hand-mades and furnishings that attract owner Cassandra Hughes because "they celebrate flights of fancy." Her store decor mixes antiques with new designs for a touch of home.

HANNAH'S TREASURES

1101 Seventh Street

Harlan, IA 51537

(712) 755-3173

Always enamored of nineteenth-century bandboxes, Marilyn Krehbiel fashions her own vintage-style boxes of pasteboard and covers them with antique wallpapers. She also carries other specially made gifts at her corner store on the town square in Harlan, Iowa.

JEANNE VAN ETTEN

Main Street

New Preston, CT 06777

(860) 868-0356

Once Jeanne Van Etten's design ideas filled her studio to capacity, she decided to catch the overflow by opening a gift shop. Her appealing doodles can now be found on stationery, pottery, and china.

MAISON DU CHARM

331 South Pineapple Street

Sarasota, FL 34236

(941) 906-7431

Surrounding herself with all things French, Madeline Lyons has furnished her shop in the sunny designs of the French countryside. From fabric to furniture, pillows to prints, French provincial decor is what defines her store and sets it apart.

MANHATTAN FRUITIER

105 East Twenty-ninth Street

New York, NY 10016

(800) 841-5718   www.manhattanfruitier.com

Artfully arranged fruit baskets overflowing with the season's best fresh bounty are the trademark of Manhattan Fruitier. The baskets might also contain a bottle of sparkling cider or a box of chocolates, depending on the occasion.

PAINTED PIG

278 Fillmore Street

Denver, CO 80206

(303) 333-2648

Wendy Grossman's painted pieces are the headliners at her Denver store, where garden and home accessories round out the selection. Wendy applies her paintbrush to vases, frames, and mirrors, transforming them into one-of-a-kind gifts.

TAIL OF THE YAK

2632 Ashby Avenue

Berkeley, CA 94705

(510) 841-9891

In a tiny cottage that blooms inside and out, treasures are to be found everywhere—in glass-fronted display cases and curio cabinets, on plant stands and pedestals. Tail of the Yak's selection of jewelry, silk flowers, ribbons, and trims is right at home here—until customers find homes for the items themselves.

Museum Shops

BLITHEWOLD MANSION, GARDEN, AND ARBORETUM

101 Ferry Road, Route 114

Bristol, RI 02809-0716

(401) 253-2707   info@heritagetrust.org

A forty-five-room summer "cottage," magnificent gardens set

on thirty-three acres of land, and an arboretum draw visitors to Blithewold. But don't miss a visit to the gift shop, where books, seeds, and birdhouses continue the property's nature theme.

....

BRAMAH TEA MUSEUM

1 Maguire Street

London SC1 2NQ England

(011) 44 171 378 0222

The best possible roundup of teas, coffees, and related paraphernalia is available at this gift shop, allowing visitors to take home a souvenir of their trip to a museum devoted entirely to tea.

....

DORFLINGER GLASS MUSEUM

Long Ridge Road

White Mills, PA 18473

(717) 253-1185   dglassmus@aol.com   www.dorflinger.org

In a former farmhouse dedicated to the art of glass, crystal reigns supreme. At both the Dorflinger Museum and its attendant gift shop, eye-catching pieces of glassware are on display, some as part of the museum's collection, others for buying and taking home.

....

HENRY B. PLANT MUSEUM

401 West Kennedy Boulevard

Tampa, FL 33606

(813) 254-1891   www.plantmuseum.com

The gilded age is still in full swing at Tampa's Henry B. Plant Museum, a former home built by the railroad tycoon in the 1880s and now a newly restored museum. The museum store's wares match the opulence of the day.

....

ISABELLA STEWART GARDNER MUSEUM

28 The Fenway

Boston, MA 02115

(617) 566-1401   www.boston.com/gardner

Arts patron Isabella Stewart Gardner built her Italianate palazzo in Boston at the turn of the century as both a home and a museum. Now it serves as a setting for her collection of artwork on display for public viewing. The museum's gift shop continues Isabella's commitment to fine art and design with books, jewelry, cards, and tableware.

....

MONTICELLO, HOME OF THOMAS JEFFERSON

P.O. Box 316

Charlottesville, VA 22902

(804) 984-9800   www.monticello.org

Monticello, Virginia, home of Thomas Jefferson, was the former president's lifelong love and endeavor. He designed the house and gardens to reflect his interests and pursuits. The Monticello gift shop pays homage to those interests by choosing merchandise that matches Jefferson's sensibilities.

....

NATIONAL MUSEUM OF WOMEN IN THE ARTS

1250 New York Avenue NW

Washington, DC 20005

(202) 783-5000   www.nmwa.org

   In 1987 a museum dedicated solely to women artists opened in Washington, DC, thanks to the passionate efforts of collector Wilhelmina Holladay. The National Museum of Women in the Arts is a pioneering success, as is its gift shop, also promoting the works of women artists.

WINTERTHUR MUSEUM

Winterthur, DE 19735

(800) 448-3883   www.winterthur.org

   One of the finest museums in the country, Winterthur is a treat to visit any time of the year. And no visit is complete without a stop at the museum's gift shop, offering items that enrich one's appreciation of fine design. Many of the designs in the store are reproduced from the Winterthur collection.